MW01613420

Unlocking the Power of Your Thinking

John W. Stanko

urbanpress

Unlocking the Power of Your Thinking
by John W. Stanko

ISBN 978-1-63360-173-4

For Worldwide Distribution
Printed in the U.S.A.

Urban Press
P.O. Box 8881
Pittsburgh, PA 15221-0881
412.646.2780

Table of Contents

Introduction

When I began writing the *Monday Memo* in 2001, I usually wrote about a different subject every week. However, over the last few years, I have been writing *Memos* that are part of an ongoing theme so I can turn them into a book when the theme has run its course. That's how I wrote most of the content in my four books in the *Unlocking* series, along with

- *Go and Obey: God's Call to Action*
- *Put Me In, Coach: Living a Bold Life*
- *Success in Babylon; How to Thrive in a Hostile Spiritual World*
- *The Power of Purple: Women of Purpose in Scripture*
- *The Proverbs 31 Man: Brothers of Purpose in Scripture*

Speaking of the *Unlocking* series, this will be the fifth in what I hope is a six-part series of books to help you live a productive and purposeful life. This *Unlocking* will be added to

- *Unlocking the Power of Your Purpose*
- *Unlocking the Power of Your Creativity*
- *Unlocking the Power of Your Productivity*
- *Unlocking the Power of You*

The sixth and final volume in the series will be *Unlocking the Power of Your Faith* currently in the works.

WHAT TO EXPECT

All my *Unlocking* books have 52 short chapters so readers can study one every week for a year or read through the book at a faster or slower pace. What's more, none of the *Unlocking* books are written in a linear fashion. In other words, I jump from subject to subject so readers can feel free to do the same, reading chapter 14 today and 39 tomorrow.

While this *Unlocking* will follow the format of the others, it focuses on a special topic of vital importance for every believer. Even though our thinking and resulting thoughts play an important role in our spiritual growth and development, the very topic of thoughts and thinking is fraught with controversy and there are more than a few theories as to their relevance and role in our spiritual lives.

Some believe we are only receivers of ideas from another source, like the Spirit or the devil, as they "drop" thoughts and ideas into our pliable and receptive brains. Others subscribe to the name-it-and-claim-it philosophy, which says if we think it and proclaim it long enough, we will receive it. Then there is the closely related positive thinking camp where we are taught to think happy thoughts if we want to be happy (I know that is an over generalization of each one of those categories). And some are simply nervous that any discussion of cognitive matters is dangerously close to New Age philosophy—you may be among any or all of those camps where *epistemology* is concerned. (I thought I would throw out a big word, but don't be intimidated. *Epistemology* is simply the study of knowledge—where it comes from and the role it has in our behavior. Any study of knowledge has to include thinking.)

I have had no greater or more important breakthrough in my life over the last 15 years than in the area of my thought life. I've learned how to remove the limitations I imposed on myself and God by confronting and changing my thoughts to align with God's will for me. I have learned much about these two passages of Scripture where our thought life is concerned:

> Therefore, I urge you, brothers and sisters, in view of God's mercy, to offer your bodies as a living sacrifice, holy and pleasing to God—this is your true and proper worship. Do not conform to the pattern of this world, but be transformed by the renewing of your mind. Then you will be able to test and approve what God's will is—his good, pleasing and perfect will (Romans 12:1-2).
>
> For though we live in the world, we do not wage war

> as the world does. The weapons we fight with are not the weapons of the world. On the contrary, they have divine power to demolish strongholds. We demolish arguments and every pretension that sets itself up against the knowledge of God, and we take captive every thought to make it obedient to Christ. And we will be ready to punish every act of disobedience, once your obedience is complete (2 Corinthians 10:3-6).

The activity of the mind we are to renew is our thinking, which means if we want the transformation that comes from being a spiritual being in right relationship with God, then we must engage the Spirit at the level of our thoughts. He does not want to transform us from outside our being but inside. Don't say "amen" to that last statement too quickly, for most of us have believed if we got a touch from the Spirit outside of us through prayer or others or His sovereign move in our lives, then we would and could be transformed. I wish it was that easy.

The passage from 2 Corinthians seems to imply from the context that taking thoughts captive to the obedience of Christ involves some measure of warfare. That indicates the process is not easy and our success is not guaranteed. Thoughts we have developed and nurtured for decades will not go away in a day. Fears and attitudes will not melt in the presence of God unless we take specific steps to enhance and enable the process, as Paul described:

> Those who live according to the flesh have their minds set on what the flesh desires; but those who live in accordance with the Spirit have their minds set on what the Spirit desires. The mind governed by the flesh is death, but the mind governed by the Spirit is life and peace. The mind governed by the flesh is hostile to God; it does not submit to God's law, nor can it do so. Those who are in the realm of the flesh cannot please God . . . Therefore, brothers and sisters, we have an obligation—but it is not to the flesh, to live according to it. For if you live according to the flesh, you will die; but if by the

> Spirit you put to death the misdeeds of the body, you will live (Romans 8:5-8, 12-13).

We are to utilize the Spirit's help in putting to death the misdeeds of the body and one of those misdeeds is thinking that sets itself on the "flesh desires." What are those flesh desires? I choose not to get into that here, but it seems to be anything that does not contribute to what Paul described as "life and peace."

In this fifth book in the *Unlocking* series, I want to share what I have learned because I now realize if the other unlockings are to take place (if you are to unlock the power of your purpose, creativity, productivity, personality, or faith), then you will need to learn or perhaps re-learn how to think.

Let me give you a warning as I close this Introduction: memorizing Scripture is *not* the way to renew or unlock your thinking. I know many people who have memorized "God has not given us a spirit of fear" (2 Timothy 1:7) but then live in terror that they will fail or even succeed. I know others who can quote verses on hospitality, generosity, and missions, but who are not involved in any of them (and of course, I am guilty of the same). Therefore, we must learn how to allow memorized Scripture verses to actually change our thoughts and then our behaviors if God's word is to have its rightful place not only in our hearts but also our minds.

There you have what you will be reading in the pages that follow. Read it with an open mind (that is another key to unlocking the power of your thinking, which is to examine your thoughts and adjust them where they may be faulty or incomplete). Keep a journal of what you learn and then perform surgery on your thoughts with the Spirit's help so the life and peace Paul mentioned will be yours in abundance. And of course, there will be plenty of tips on how to apply your new thinking to the topic of my life's work for the last three decades—how to find your life purpose.

John W. Stanko
Pittsburgh, PA
August 2021

"Whatever is true, whatever is noble, whatever is right, whatever is pure, whatever is lovely, whatever is admirable—if anything is excellent or praiseworthy—think about such things" (Philippians 4:8).

Week #1

Taking Thoughts Captive

I have known for some time that I have a mental health challenge and I'm learning to confront it on a daily basis. That's the good news. The bad news is you have the same mental health condition, but your good news is you can deal with it just like I am. Let's examine this "problem" together as we begin our study of how to unlock the power of your thinking.

The Problem

Here is a definition of mental illness I retrieved from the National Alliance on Mental Illness:

> A mental illness is a condition that affects a person's thinking, feeling or mood. Such conditions may affect someone's ability to relate to others and function every day. Each person will have different experiences, even people with the same diagnosis. Recovery, including meaningful roles in social life, school and work, is possible, especially when you start treatment early and play a strong role in your own recovery process. A mental health condition isn't the result of one event. Research suggests multiple, linking causes. Genetics, environment and lifestyle influence whether someone develops a mental health condition. A stressful job or home life makes some people more susceptible, as do traumatic life events like being the victim of a crime. Biochemical processes and circuits and basic brain structure may play a role, too.

Notice the first line: "A mental illness is a condition that affects a person's thinking, feeling or mood." I agree with most of what the rest of the paragraph says is true, but I would disagree with one point. The experts say that "a mental health condition isn't the result of one event." I would argue that it is the result of a single event and that event is known as our Fall in the Garden. When Adam and Eve decided to eat from the tree of the knowledge of good and evil, they unleashed the cause of my mental condition (and yours).

Even when my mental condition may be caused by genetics or a faulty brain function, I can trace that problem back to the Fall, for God did not create man with any defects (He declared what He had made was "good"). Sinful thinking was my problem, is my problem, and will continue to be my problem, and I dare say the same is true for you. My thinking has been so wrong for so long that when I decide to confront it, I'm facing a lifetime of accumulated wrong thoughts. The good news is the Spirit is with me when I start to rebuild my thought inventory as I mentioned in the Introduction:

> Those who live according to the flesh have their minds set on what the flesh desires; but those who live in accordance with the Spirit have their minds set on what the Spirit desires. The mind governed by the flesh is death, but the mind governed by the Spirit is life and peace. The mind governed by the flesh is hostile to God; it does not submit to God's law, nor can it do so. Those who are in the realm of the flesh cannot please God. You, however, are not in the realm of the flesh but are in the realm of the Spirit, if indeed the Spirit of God lives in you. And if anyone does not have the Spirit of Christ, they do not belong to Christ (Romans 8:5-9)

I realize there are some genetic defects or injuries that hinder or prevent normal brain functioning, and I am not addressing those. My point is the main function of our mental capacity is to think and that function has been impaired and reinforced through what I deem wrong or bad thinking, which has impacted my moods, attitudes, and behavior.

My Thinking, Your Thinking

Isn't your thinking the source of your feelings and moods?

Isn't your thinking the source of yours (and my) addictions to shopping, anger, fear, and/or anti-social behavior? Paul wrote a helpful passage regarding our thinking in 2 Corinthians 10:4-6:

> The weapons we fight with are not the weapons of the world. On the contrary, they have divine power to demolish strongholds. We demolish arguments and every pretension that sets itself up against the knowledge of God, and we take captive every thought to make it obedient to Christ. And we will be ready to punish every act of disobedience, once your obedience is complete.

In those verses, Paul introduced another possible cause for my mental condition and that is demonic activity. My thoughts that lead to my moods and behaviors can have their origins in supernatural powers that want to keep me enslaved and prevent me from obeying God. All this wrong thinking requires some measure of resistance on my part if it is to be made right, as our definition above stated as well: We must play a "strong role" in our own recovery process. Paul would agree and say we must take every one of our thoughts captive to the obedience of God's word in the power of the Spirit. Our willingness has to be present for the Spirit to be effective in doing that.

For me to play a role in my recovery, I must be aware of my thoughts—I have to think about and reflect on what I am thinking about. I must put my thoughts under the microscope, send them off for lab results, or put them through a series of x-rays to determine if they are the source of my mental condition that is hindering my effectiveness and relationships with others—and God. When I find they are, then I must wrestle and fight a spiritual battle to change those thoughts. If I take a "strong role" in the power of the Spirit, I can reverse this mental condition, which seems to be a lifetime process as I walk out my faith in Christ.

I am not opposing or denying the diagnosis of my problem, and I urge you not to resist yours as well. I am the source of my own problems, but I can hasten my healing by not fighting the diagnosis or the cure, and that cure is aligning my thoughts with

God's thoughts—thus unlocking the power of my thinking as God intended. The Spirit came to give me the mind of Christ, and I must be aware that this does not come naturally or easily, but only through spiritual effort free from my tendency to control the process. I must stop eating from the tree of the knowledge of good and evil and feast on the fruit from the tree of life. When that happens, my diet of right thinking will deliver me from my condition, and it will do the same for you.

Week #2

A Stronghold Has a Strong Hold

Let's examine exactly what a stronghold is since we often refer to it as something we must pull down. We can assume it as something "out there," like an evil institution or practice, but let's consider the possibility it is something "in here"—in your mind that may be hindering your spiritual growth and progress.

RENEWING THE MIND

Let's start off by considering two passages I used as the basis for a message I once preached in my home church:

> "Therefore, I urge you, brothers and sisters, in view of God's mercy, to offer your bodies as a living sacrifice, holy and pleasing to God—this is your true and proper worship. Do not conform to the pattern of this world, but be transformed by the renewing of your mind. Then you will be able to test and approve what God's will is—his good, pleasing and perfect will" (Romans 12:1-2).

> "For though we live in the world, we do not wage war as the world does. The weapons we fight with are not the weapons of the world. On the contrary, they have divine power to demolish strongholds. We demolish arguments and every pretension that sets itself up against the knowledge of God, and we take captive every thought to make it obedient to Christ" (2 Corinthians 10:3-5).

Can there be a stronghold that has a strong hold on our minds? The answer is yes. A stronghold is an accumulation of thoughts and beliefs over time that become established ways of doing things or seeing the world. For example, if as a child you did not do well in math, you begin to think, "I'm just not good at math." That thought is reinforced by poor performance, which just "proves" you are not smart where math is concerned. Perhaps comments from others reinforced the thought even further, so therefore you began to dread or avoid math classes.

When you got to university and were confronted with having to take a math class, panic set in because you knew how you are. The thought had become a stronghold in your mind, telling you again and again you are no good at math. Even though your parents worked with you and encouraged you, even prayed for you, the stronghold remained and it affected your performance. It continued to grow and spread its roots, so even though you excelled at other subjects, you were not capable of doing well at math.

Another stronghold could be your ability or need to use social media: "Oh, I'm no good at that. I don't have time anyway. It's also such a waste of time." As the world continues to go digital and connects through many media, you resist the trend because you have a stronghold that actually causes you to fear or loathe social media. You may not act like you are afraid, maintaining it is your choice not to participate. You may even reinforce your position with biblical truths, but in most cases, you have built up a thought that now has a strong hold on your mind. Once you put a stronghold behind a biblical or religious fortress, it becomes even more difficult to identify, confront, and change, which is what we are really trying to do when we "tear it down."

STRONGHOLDS AND FEAR

The thing I saw for the first time when I preached from these two passages is that a stronghold in your mind *always* results in panic and fear when that stronghold is challenged or confronted, just like the life examples I provided above. An example of this truth about fear can be seen in the story of David and Goliath. The army had a collective stronghold in their minds, which was that Goliath was too big for anyone to fight and defeat. When Goliath's presence confronted their stronghold, they were terrified: "On hearing the Philistine's words, Saul and all the Israelites were dismayed and terrified" (1 Samuel 17:11) and "whenever the

Israelites saw the man, they all fled from him in great fear" (1 Samuel 17:24).

You can memorize all the Scripture verses you want but if, for instance, there is cancer in your family and the thought you will get cancer has a strong hold on your mind, you will live in fear. Studies also show the stronghold can actually lead to the thing you fear becoming a reality! That's why it's important to identify your strongholds and deal with them, one by one. I have determined I am to be on a search-and-destroy mission for my remaining days to identify my fear strongholds and bring them down.

How can you tear down your strongholds? You can do so first by honestly assessing where your greatest fears are. Where do you have a firmly entrenched fear that seems rational but limits your faith and then your walk? The opposite of fear is not unbelief; it is faith, so a stronghold keeps you from acting in faith, Since faith is how you please God and your fear won't allow you to function in faith, your stronghold is a barrier to obeying and pleasing God—in faith.

Once you acknowledge a stronghold has a strong hold on your life, you can then begin the process of dismantling, disarming, and replacing it. The Spirit will help you do this, but there are no shortcuts. You must work to undo what it has taken years to build. In the next chapter, we will look further into how you can pull down a stronghold, but your assignment this week is to get comfortable with the fact that you have some of them and analyze the effects they produce in your life. Then get ready for the demolition process as you face their existence, examine how they got so strong and well entrenched, and determine they must go.

Week #3

How to Build a Strong Stronghold

As we pursue the process that will allow you to unlock the power of your thinking as God intends, the path to this process is littered with debris from teachings labeled "name it and claim it," "positive thinking," and "mind over matter." It would make sense, however, that a topic of this importance would have opposition and a variety of counterfeits and halfway measures. No one ever makes phony $4 bills because there are no real $4 bills. There is only value in producing a fake that has some basis in truth and reality. That is the reason I have chosen to write about how God made our brain to function and how we can use it to work with Him and not against Him—to expose the counterfeit and value the real.

In the last chapter, we looked at a stronghold and I promised this week we would look at how to pull down a stronghold. Rather than study how to deal with a counterfeit stronghold, I thought I would share how to build a proper one. Let's get started.

BUILD ONE

In the last chapter, I defined a stronghold as "an accumulation of thoughts and beliefs over time that become established ways of doing things or seeing the world." Let me decribe how I built what I consider a positive stronghold to help you do the same. Then in the next chapter, we will look at how to demolish a negative one.

About 40 years ago, I was diagnosed with a bad back. My mother had suffered with back problems so it made sense to me that I could have inherited this condition from her. I was told by a doctor it was just a matter of time before I would need surgery to correct a structural problem. I was presented with a thought and had a choice to either build a supportive cast of thoughts that would reinforce that diagnosis or build an alternative collection that would focus on healing. I figured I had nothing to lose by choosing to build a positive stronghold around healing. If I was wrong, I would have gone off chasing an idle pursuit and just have the surgery. If I was right, there were obvious benefits. From that day forward, I decided to trust God for my healing, even though I was in pain. I read and meditated on Exodus 15:26:

> "If you listen carefully to the Lord your God and do what is right in his eyes, if you pay attention to his commands and keep all his decrees, I will not bring on you any of the diseases I brought on the Egyptians, *for I am the Lord, who heals you*" (emphasis added).

It was not debilitating pain and I continued with my life pretty much as normal, assured by my doctor that playing sports, working in my garden, or other normal activities would not cause further damage. Every summer I would play softball, go to the chiropractor the next day, and thank God for my healing. This went on for years. I would be in the shower or in the car and when I would feel the pain, I would thank God for my healing.

A SLIP UP

After many years of doing this, my wife and I were on a cruise with the ministry I was working for at the time. We were walking down a corridor to a meeting when I stepped on a piece of celery from a reception that had just been held in the area. My one leg went flying into the air and I fell landing on my back, at which point I began to shout, "Thank You, Lord! Thank You, Lord!" People thought I was injured but the opposite was true. For the first time I realized my back didn't hurt. I could not say when the pain left, but the pain that should have resulted from that fall was absent—and had been gone for a while without me noticing. That fall took place in 1994 and I have had no problems since.

I did not allow the thought of surgery to get a strong hold in my mind. Instead, I built a stronghold that God is my Healer, reinforcing and surrounding that thought with other thoughts consistent with my starting point. I have used that model to build other strongholds to guide my thinking and behavior, such as "I can write more than one book a year." "God doesn't need a company to pay me. He can do that Himself." "I can have energy and be productive until I die at a ripe old age." As with my healing mindset, if I'm wrong, what have I really lost? If I'm on the right path, however, I have much to gain.

In the next chapter, we will examine how to tear down and replace a negative stronghold, but the process involves what I described this week. You must find a new thought that will become the foundation or pillar of your belief and build a supportive mental structure or scaffolding around it. For now, you can start to build a positive, godly stronghold by accepting a simple truth and choosing to believe it, no matter how much opposition it receives from conflicting thoughts that assail your mind. Your job will be to find thoughts and Bible verses that can partner with your new thought. While you do that, I'm going to once again bend over and thank God for His healing power that proved stronger and mightier than a doctor's prognosis.

Week #4

How to Build a Better Stronghold

Have you ever thought or said, "If God would only speak to me or show me a sign, then I would know and do His will"? There is nothing wrong with that, except if you have a thought that conflicts with what God is trying to say, then you may not be able to hear it as you assumed you would. Let's take a look in this chapter at how a stronghold gains such a strong hold in your life and how you can replace it with another better and stronger one.

KILL AND EAT

If I tell you not to think about a pink elephant, that is exactly what you will continue to think about and visualize. You cannot simply stop thinking about something that has a grip on your mind, especially if it has also become part of your worldview and life philosophy. You established that thought or network of thoughts over time through concerted and repetitive effort, so it will take some time and work to pull it down and replace it. Let's look at how Peter replaced a stronghold in his mind as an example from which we can learn. We read,

> About noon the following day as they were on their journey and approaching the city, Peter went up on the roof to pray. He became hungry and wanted something to eat, and while the meal was being prepared, he fell into a trance. He saw heaven opened and something like a large sheet being let down to earth by its four corners. It contained all kinds of four-footed animals, as well as reptiles and birds. Then a voice told him, "Get up, Peter. Kill and eat." "Surely not, Lord!" Peter replied. "I have never eaten anything impure or unclean." The voice spoke to him a second time, "Do not call anything

> impure that God has made clean." This happened three times, and immediately the sheet was taken back to heaven (Acts 10:9-16).

Peter was raised as a kosher Jew, only eating food declared clean by God's word. That thought had become a way of life and a stronghold in his mind. Then he had a vision telling him to eat unclean things and he naturally resisted, telling the Lord he would *never* do that—because Peter did not believe the Lord would direct him to do so.

Right after Peter had the vision, some men appeared where he was lodging and invited him to come to Cornelius' home. Peter went, saw the Holy Spirit fall on the Gentiles, and only then realized God was speaking to him. The result was to be a new way of thinking or a new stronghold:

> "As I began to speak, the Holy Spirit came on them as he had come on us at the beginning. Then I remembered what the Lord had said: 'John baptized with water, but you will be baptized with the Holy Spirit.' So if God gave them the same gift he gave us who believed in the Lord Jesus Christ, *who was I to think that I could stand in God's way*?" (Acts 11:15-17, emphasis added).

TRANSFORMED BY A MIND RENEWAL

Peter asked those who challenged what he did, "Who was I to think I could stand in God's way?" That certainly hadn't stopped other Jewish leaders, for they thought they could stand in God's way when they didn't believe it was God's way—which is why they tried to eliminate Jesus. Peter decided to change his thinking and was transformed into a man who welcomed Samaritans and Gentiles into the Kingdom because he allowed God to give him a new thought and he built a support system around it: "Do not conform to the pattern of this world, but be transformed by the renewing of your mind. Then you will be able to test and approve what God's will is—his good, pleasing and perfect will" (Romans 12:2). How did this happen to Peter? It happened with the Spirit's help:

> Those who live according to the flesh have their minds set on what the flesh desires; but those who live in accordance with the Spirit have their minds set on what the Spirit desires. The mind governed by the flesh is death, but the mind governed by the Spirit is life and peace. The mind governed by the flesh is hostile to God; it does not submit to God's law, nor can it do so. Those who are in the realm of the flesh cannot please God. You, however, are not in the realm of the flesh but are in the realm of the Spirit, if indeed the Spirit of God lives in you. And if anyone does not have the Spirit of Christ, they do not belong to Christ (Romans 8:5-9).

However, you must be careful not to over-spiritualize this process. Even though the Spirit was involved, Peter had to cooperate with the Spirit's work. He had to be open to the fact that his old stronghold was wrong or at least incomplete or inadequate. He had to have courage to consider the new thought by examining the vision, the visitors, and his encounter with Cornelius and then come to and announce a new conclusion—allowing that conclusion to build a network of supporting thoughts in his mind that God was welcoming Gentiles into His kingdom.

What steps can you take to build a new stronghold? It's quite simple:

1. Accept the fact that you cannot see or know it all and that you may be wrong or only partially correct where your current conclusions are concerned.
2. Listen to others, even those who hold a different view, without obligation to agree or determination to refute.
3. Search the Scriptures without assuming you know what something means. In other words, be open to see what you have not seen.

If you do your part, I promise God will do His and the Spirit, whose job it is to lead and guide you into all the truth, will empower you to be transformed not by some supernatural encounter but through the power of new thoughts. Then you will have the courage to discover, confront, and replace other strongholds in your mind so you can be constantly transformed into a vessel for God's purposes.

Week #5

Figure it Out

Let's continue to examine how you can unlock the power of your thinking by looking once again at the story of Peter and his visit to Cornelius in Acts 10 that we began to look at in week four.

TWO VISIONS

The story of how Cornelius and his household came to know the Lord and receive the Holy Spirit focuses on two separate visions. Here is the first:

> One day at about three in the afternoon he had a vision. He distinctly saw an angel of God, who came to him and said, "Cornelius!" Cornelius stared at him in fear. "What is it, Lord?" he asked. The angel answered, "Your prayers and gifts to the poor have come up as a memorial offering before God. Now send men to Joppa to bring back a man named Simon who is called Peter. He is staying with Simon the tanner, whose house is by the sea" (Acts 10:3-6).

Notice how straightforward this vision was. Cornelius was told *exactly* what to do, where to go, and who to summon. There was no room for misinterpretation unless Cornelius wasn't paying attention or didn't want to follow through, neither of which were true. Then we learn of Peter's vision:

> About noon the following day as they were on their journey and approaching the city, Peter went up on the roof to pray. He became hungry and wanted something to eat, and while the meal was being prepared, he fell into a trance. He saw heaven opened and something like a large sheet being let down to earth by its four

> corners. It contained all kinds of four-footed animals, as well as reptiles and birds. Then a voice told him, "Get up, Peter. Kill and eat." "Surely not, Lord!" Peter replied. "I have never eaten anything impure or unclean." The voice spoke to him a second time, "Do not call anything impure that God has made clean." This happened three times, and immediately the sheet was taken back to heaven (Acts 10:9-16).

Notice that Peter's vision was not so straightforward. It was full of symbols and did not directly portray the issue God was addressing in his life. In one case, there were clear directions; in the other, there was ambiguity that left room for interpretation. Why the difference?

FIGURE IT OUT

The reason is that Peter had more of a spiritual history with Jesus than Cornelius did. Therefore, Jesus expected Peter to consider what he saw in his vision and the chain of events that followed to come to the conclusion he ultimately did: "I now realize how true it is that God does not show favoritism but accepts from every nation the one who fears him and does what is right" (Acts 10:34). Peter had to observe, process, and allow the Holy Spirit to persuade and convince him of the truth (which Jesus had said was one of the Spirit's roles). Peter did and unlocked the power of his thinking to come to a knowledge of the truth. You must learn to do the same.

I have often heard people say, "If God would only speak to me" and I certainly believe He does speak to people. I have also come to realize, however, that when He speaks, we may still have a role in figuring out what He said. When He speaks literally, it is not necessarily a sign of our spirituality, but more so of our immaturity as was the case with Cornelius. Later in Acts, when Paul and his company were trying to move on in their missionary work, the Spirit was blocking their path. Then one night Paul had a dream:

> During the night Paul had a vision of a man of Macedonia standing and begging him, "Come over to

> Macedonia and help us." After Paul had seen the vision, we got ready at once to leave for Macedonia, *concluding that God had called us to preach the gospel to them* (Acts 16:9-10, emphasis added).

What did Paul and his team do after Paul had the dream? They figured out what God was saying and "concluded" they were to go to Macedonia, which was in the opposite direction of where they had been trying to go. Please don't misunderstand, I'm not suggesting we walk in our own understanding, but I am saying the Spirit's presence in our lives is there to help us have the mind of Christ. That means we must learn not only to think God's thoughts, but also to cooperate with God's thought process.

The older we are in the Lord, the more we are expected to interpret and think through the plans or words God has for us. However, the older we get, the more set in our ways of thinking we can be and thus find ourselves who were involved in a previous move of God to be resisting the next move of God because it does not fit our mental model.

The objective of this book is to get you past the fear and doubt that cause you to think God is trying to trick you. Also, you must learn to have a pliable and flexible mind when it comes to serving the Lord and understanding His will for your life. God is at work within you no matter how long you have known Him, and your thinking plays an important role in being transformed into His image as well as becoming an obedient, fruitful, and creative servant. I hope this week you will spend some time trying to "figure out" what the Lord is saying with confidence that the Spirit is there to help and not hinder you from achieving the right path. Once you figure it out, cooperate with the process and finish the job of building a new stronghold that will cooperate with and not resist the will of God.

Week #6

Mind Your Mind

In this chapter, let's look at a few verses in Paul's letter to the Philippians that relate to the topic of your mind and thoughts.

THINK ABOUT YOUR THOUGHTS

Paul instructed us concerning our thinking throughout the letter to his favorite church, using the word *mind* five times:

- . . . then make my joy complete by being like-minded, having the same love, being one in spirit and of one mind (2:2).
- In your relationships with one another, have the same mindset as Christ Jesus (2:5).
- Their destiny is destruction, their god is their stomach, and their glory is in their shame. Their mind is set on earthly things (3:19).
- I plead with Euodia and I plead with Syntyche to be of the same mind in the Lord (4:2).
- And the peace of God, which transcends all understanding, will guard your hearts and your minds in Christ Jesus (4:7).

The last verse is part of a passage that will now be our focus:

> Rejoice in the Lord always. I will say it again: Rejoice! Let your gentleness be evident to all. The Lord is near. Do not be anxious about anything, but in every situation, by prayer and petition, with thanksgiving, present your requests to God. And the peace of God, which transcends all understanding, will guard your hearts and your minds in Christ Jesus. Finally, brothers and

> sisters, whatever is true, whatever is noble, whatever is right, whatever is pure, whatever is lovely, whatever is admirable—if anything is excellent or praiseworthy—think about such things. Whatever you have learned or received or heard from me, or seen in me—put it into practice. And the God of peace will be with you (Philippians 4:4-9).

In essence, Paul was instructing us to mind our mind or think about our thoughts throughout his letter. In Philippians 4, he was addressing a squabble between two women and fellow gospel workers, Euodia and Syntyche. It's of note that he did not spell out the problem or try to adjudicate it. Instead, Paul urged then all to get their minds focused on the right things and off the source of their contention.

If they wanted peace, then Paul showed them they must keep their minds thinking thoughts that were lovely, admirable, excellent, praiseworthy, and pure. Paul wasn't simply urging them not to think about their differences. He was teaching them to "make those things the subject of your thoughtful consideration, carefully reflecting on them" (*Vine's Dictionary of Old and New Testament Words*).

THE MIND OF CHRIST

In Philippians 2:5, Paul told his readers to "have the same mindset as Christ." Is that even possible? We have often been taught that our minds and hearts are cesspools, prone to wander into enemy territory and thus lead us astray. Paul wasn't buying into that thinking and ordered his disciples to have the mind and attitude of Christ. He was not telling his readers to empty their minds so God could fill them. He was advising them to "reckon, calculate, and reason out those things to serve God and men" (*Vine's*).

In other words, Paul told us to find a godly thought and chew on, dwell, focus on, develop, and turn it over again and again. We will hear from God when we stop waiting for Him to "drop" thoughts into our minds and thinking about whatever comes to mind until that happens. We are to play an active role in what occupies our mind by filling it with good things—otherwise we are prone to the problem the two women had in the Philippian church. We will each decide what is right and insist others comply and agree and if they don't, then we will consider them "wrong" and argue to make them "right."

I have discovered after 47 years of ministry that most people have trouble hearing from the Lord to determine God's will for them. The reason isn't because they are unspiritual or don't want to know. It's because they have not minded their mind. They waste their mind energy on anxiety, worry, fantasies, hurts, and daydreams, which are all junk food for the brain. That junk works against the mind of the Spirit and crowds out the thoughts of God.

If you want to unlock the power of your thinking, then you must take an active role and replace the negative with the spiritual. You must also heed Paul's words and teaching in Philippians. If you do that and mind your mind and think about your thoughts, Paul promised you will have peace. If you choose, like Adam and Eve, to decide for yourself what thoughts you will keep and develop, you will fall short of God's best for your life.

Paul would not have commanded us to have the mindset of Christ if it wasn't possible to have in the power of the Spirit. I encourage you to meditate on this subject this week and determine once and for all to have the mind of Christ. You do your part, which is honestly assessing your state of mind, and then enlist the Spirit's help as you clean house. Don't just tear down old thoughts but be sure to replace them with thoughts that meet the criteria spelled out in Philippians 4:8-9. When you do, you will unlock much of the spiritual power you have desired but lacked up to this point in time.

Week #7

A Word From the Lord

Have you ever wished God would speak to you face-to-face so you could know what to do? Have you ever said, "I need a word from the Lord!"? Doesn't that sound like it would make serving and obeying God much easier? A direct encounter with God during which He spells out His will for your life didn't work for Gideon, however, and it may not work for you either—especially if your mind is focused on your less-than-ideal circumstances. Before you can hear from Him or comprehend the full impact of what He is saying, you may need to unlock the power of your thinking—the theme of this book. To prove my point, let's look at the life of Gideon in this chapter.

CAN WE TALK?

One day Gideon was busy trying to eke out a living when the Lord appeared and spoke to him:

> The angel of the Lord came and sat down under the oak in Ophrah that belonged to Joash the Abiezrite, where his son Gideon was threshing wheat in a winepress to keep it from the Midianites. When the angel of the Lord appeared to Gideon, he said, "The Lord is with you, mighty warrior." "Pardon me, my lord," Gideon replied, "but if the Lord is with us, why has all this happened to us? Where are all his wonders that our ancestors told us about when they said, 'Did not the Lord bring us up out of Egypt?' But now the Lord has abandoned us and given us into the hand of Midian" (Judges 6:11-13).

What was Gideon's response? Was he in awe and didn't know what to say? Did he worship? Did he ask the Lord for more specifics about what He wanted him to do? No, he did none of those things. Instead, he basically said, "Can we talk?" Gideon took the opportunity to complain and tell the Lord how bad things were in his life. Gideon had a direct word and appearance from the Lord, but he was so preoccupied with his situation that he didn't treat them like the special events they were. What's more, he told the Lord how misguided He was to choose him. Fortunately, that did not deter the Lord, who went on to reveal why He had come and what He wanted Gideon to do:

> The Lord turned to him and said, "Go in the strength you have and save Israel out of Midian's hand. Am I not sending you?" "But Lord," Gideon asked, "how can I save Israel? My clan is the weakest in Manasseh, and I am the least in my family" (Judges 6:14-15).

Once again, Gideon turned God's directive into a time to complain, telling the Lord why he could not be the one to do what the Lord was directing. This is a good example of how your thinking can work *against* hearing and doing God's will, which is why Paul pointed out that doing God's will and personal transformation both hinge on changing the way you think: "Do not conform to the pattern of this world, but be transformed by the renewing of your mind. Then you will be able to test and approve what God's will is—his good, pleasing and perfect will" (Romans 12:2). The business of your mind is to think, so if you are going to renew your mind, new thoughts or ways of thinking must be involved.

IT DIDN'T MATTER

It didn't matter to Gideon that he received a direct word from the Lord. He was so hung up on his circumstances and limitations that he could not see how God could use him. In reality, a visit from God almost turned into a bad experience for Gideon. I am sure *you* have *never* done what Gideon did in this instance. If you have, then you know firsthand that even a visitation from God isn't always the answer to your spiritual inactivity on uncertainty. Once you have a negative attitude, you can't hear or receive the word from the Lord you have been wanting and seeking.

This week, ask the Lord to reveal if you are acting like Gideon in any area of your life. If you are, then find out what God has been saying that you can't hear or receive because of your heart attitude or mindset. The good news is that Gideon went on from this encounter with the Lord to do great things and you will, too—but only if you change your thinking so you do not fight against but instead receive the word of the Lord for your life.

Week #8

Search and Destroy

I looked at Gideon in the last chapter and will look at his story in the next two as well. In Chapter Seven, we looked at how Gideon's thinking did not permit him to receive a word from the Lord. In fact, he argued with and complained to the Lord rather than embracing what the Lord had to say. I noted that when we say, "I need a word from the Lord," we still may not be in a place to receive or obey that word—until we change our thinking. In this chapter, let's look at a theme I have written about many times in the past and that theme is fear, which was certainly near the top of Gideon's challenges as he awakened to his life purpose and assignment from God.

THE PROOF

When we first meet Gideon, he was threshing wheat in a winepress, an unusual place for that activity. We learned early in Judges 6 why he was doing this there:

> The Israelites did evil in the eyes of the Lord, and for seven years he gave them into the hands of the Midianites. Because the power of Midian was so oppressive, the Israelites prepared shelters for themselves in mountain clefts, caves and strongholds. Whenever the Israelites planted their crops, the Midianites, Amalekites and other eastern peoples invaded the country. They camped on the land and ruined the crops all the way to Gaza and did not spare a living thing for Israel, neither sheep nor cattle nor donkeys. They came up with their livestock and their tents like swarms of locusts. It was impossible to count them or their camels; they invaded the land to ravage it. Midian so

> impoverished the Israelites that they cried out to the LORD for help (Judges 6:1-6).

It's clear Gideon was threshing his wheat in a place no one would think to look for him because he was afraid—afraid of the Midianites and their power to take away what little wheat he had:

> We then see that an angel of the Lord came to Israel because God heard their cries for help. After the Lord reveals the purpose for His visit to Gideon and after Gideon had expressed his displeasure with the way things were going, we read "Gideon replied, 'If now I have found favor in your eyes, give me a sign that it is really you talking to me. Please do not go away until I come back and bring my offering and set it before you." And the LORD said, "I will wait until you return'" (Judges 6:17-18).

When Gideon returned, the Lord said to him, "Peace! Do not be afraid. You are not going to die" (Judges 6:23). Later when the Lord directed Gideon to tear down his father's idolatrous altar, we read, "So Gideon took ten of his servants and did as the LORD told him. But because he was afraid of his family and the townspeople, he did it at night rather than in the daytime" (Judges 6:27). And then when God commissioned Gideon to attack the Midianites, He said,

> "Get up, go down against the camp, because I am going to give it into your hands. If you are afraid to attack, go down to the camp with your servant Purah and listen to what they are saying. Afterward, you will be encouraged to attack the camp" (Judges 7:9-11).

This evidence is more than enough to prove that Gideon was steeped in fear, but also shows God was with him every step of the way to help him overcome his fears. The same, my friend, is true for you.

FIND IT, 'FESS IT, FIX IT

To unlock the power of your thinking, you must allow the

Lord to help you confront and overcome your fears. First, assume you are afraid, whether you see it or know it. Second, armed with that assumption, go on a search-and-destroy mission to expose your fear. Third, recognize your fear often hides behind disguises that sound and appear to be spiritual: "I'm waiting on the Lord. I'm praying about it. I don't want to get ahead of the Lord." Fourth, ask for confirmation, like Gideon did, if you need it for what you believe the Lord is directing you to do. However, once you receive it, it's time to act and not delay any longer.

In short, you are to find, confess, and then fix your fear problem the same way Gideon did. You will have to confront your fear head on so you will know the truth and the truth can then set you free. Remember, it all starts by assuming you are afraid whether it appears that way to you or not. If you do that, then you can go looking in the recesses of your mind and heart for those long-standing fear thoughts that have kept you stymied and stagnant for lo these many years. Once you do this, it will become a way of life and you will find great freedom and satisfaction in searching out and destroying the fear that has gripped you for only God knows how long. When you are ready to accept you are afraid, then move on to the next chapter.

Week #9

No Way

Let's look at the story of Gideon one more time to see what lessons we can learn from his example to help us unlock the power of our thinking. In the last two chapters, we examined how fear had affected Gideon's thinking and also how his low self-esteem and lack of faith had prevented him from accepting God's visitation as the significant event it was. In this chapter, let's look at Gideon's mindset that screamed "no way" in every situation.

"WHO? ME?"

Gideon's attitude could also be labeled "who me?" for he was consistently reluctant to trust what God was revealing to him. Let's look at how his thinking impacted his actions with a few examples:

1. "O Lord, how shall I deliver Israel? Behold, my family is the least in Manasseh, and I am the youngest in my father's house" (Judges 6:15). Gideon had his mind made up that his birth order and the size of his clan, both of which were external and beyond his control, prevented him from doing anything significant for the Lord. Even when the Lord's messenger was standing before him informing him God was with him, he refused to believe he was the chosen one.
2. "If now I have found favor in Your sight, then show me a sign that it is You who speak with me" (Judges 6:17). Gideon could not believe he was hearing correctly so he requested a sign from the Lord that this really was His word and will. This indicates signs

and confirmations are to combat unbelief. In other words, when you ask for a sign, it is an indication your faith is lacking and not great faith.

3. "Then Gideon took ten men of his servants and did as the LORD had spoken to him; and because he was too afraid of his father's household and the men of the city to do it by day, he did it by night" (Judges 6:27). When the Lord told Gideon to tear down his father's idolatrous altar, he exhibited "who me?" thinking by doing it under the cover of darkness.
4. "If You will deliver Israel through me, as You have spoken, behold, I will put a fleece of wool on the threshing floor. If there is dew on the fleece only, and it is dry on all the ground, then I will know that You will deliver Israel through me, as You have spoken" (Judges 6:36). Still not convinced, Gideon asked for two more signs to confirm God's presence and reinforce the fact that God was with him.
5. "But if you are afraid to go down, go with Purah your servant down to the camp, and you will hear what they say; and afterward your hands will be strengthened that you may go down against the camp" (Judges 7:10-11 NASB). After all God had shown him, Gideon requested yet another confirmation, which God provided.

All that was still not enough to reverse Gideon's "who me?" or "no way" thinking. Let's look at one more incident and then describe the mindset Gideon should have had.

MORE

When Gideon finally blew the trumpet and assembled Israel to fight, we read, "The LORD said to Gideon, 'The people who are with you are too many for Me to give Midian into their hands, for Israel would become boastful, saying, 'My own power has delivered me'" (Judges 7:2). In essence, the Lord addressed this because Gideon was thinking, *There's no way I can win unless I have a larger army than my enemies*. It's similar to your thinking that says, "I need a company or organization to support and pay me. I don't have sufficient strength or wisdom or power to do what God is directing me to do." When you think like that, you wait and wait. For what? For *more—more* money, *more* people, *more* affirmation, *more* confirmation. Yet, God doesn't need more to use you. He just needs *you*, as the Lord tried to tell Gideon:

> The Lord turned to him and said, "*Go in the strength you have* and save Israel out of Midian's hand. Am I not sending you?" "Pardon me, my lord," Gideon replied, "but how can I save Israel? My clan is the weakest in Manasseh, and I am the least in my family." The LORD answered, "I will be with you, and you will strike down all the Midianites, leaving none alive" (Judges 6:14-16. emphasis added).

Go in the strength you have. That is the thinking you also must have if you are going to unlock the power of your thoughts and deploy them to do God's will rather than oppose it. You don't need more of anything right now, except more right thinking. When you have that, you will release the God who is with you as He was with Gideon who will then help you write, build, grow, proclaim, create, or organize "as one man (or woman)." This week, decide once and for all that you are finished with the "who me?" and "no way" attitude, putting it off with thoughts of "yes me!" and "God's way."

Week

#10

Fear Tactics

I know I promised we would be done with Gideon's story by now, but I need one more chapter to finish up. In this chapter, let's look at the fulfillment of God's promise and declaration that Gideon would lead God's people to victory over the Midianites, a role and promise Gideon was slow to accept.

HAVE COURAGE OR GO HOME

As you know by now, recognizing and addressing fear plays an important role if you are going to unlock the power of your thinking. Your brain, or at least your thinking, is marinated in fear and it requires a lifetime to address and unlearn the fear patterns you have both inherited and learned. We have seen this truth in Gideon's life in the last few chapters, but now let's examine the role fear played in the eventual victory Gideon experienced.

First, we read how the Lord whittled Gideon's army down from 32,000 to 300. It started with a call for volunteers: "Now announce to the army, 'Anyone who trembles with fear may turn back and leave Mount Gilead.' So twenty-two thousand men left, while ten thousand remained" (Judges 7:3).

The next step in reducing the army was only using those who "lapped their water as a dog lapped." I will not discuss the selection process here except to say it appears those who knelt were carelessly exposing themselves to an attack while those who cupped the water with their hands were more alert and ready for the unexpected. After this, the Lord had His army of 300 that would face the Midianite army many times its size.

What was the Lord thinking? Why would He do this? We saw in the last chapter He did this so Israel would not boast after the victory that their large army got the job done. They would celebrate their victory because God, and God alone, had accomplished it. Still, what was the Lord's lesson from this tactic and strategy?

Quite simply, the Lord knew the Midianites were also afraid. Even though they had a large army that had exercised power and control over Israel for years, they lived in terror. What were they afraid of? They were afraid of the usual things like starvation, losing their power over Israel, and death. The Lord used their fear to Israel's advantage by directing Gideon to do this:

> Dividing the three hundred men into three companies, he placed trumpets and empty jars in the hands of all of them, with torches inside. "Watch me," he told them. "Follow my lead. When I get to the edge of the camp, do exactly as I do. When I and all who are with me blow our trumpets, then from all around the camp blow yours and shout, 'For the Lord and for Gideon'" (Judges 7:16-18).

THE FEAR FACTOR

What was the result of this strategy? "When the three hundred trumpets sounded, the Lord caused the men throughout the camp to turn on each other with their swords. The army fled to Beth Shittah toward Zererah as far as the border of Abel Meholah near Tabbath" (Judges 7:22). All it took for the Midianites to panic was the *thought* they were under attack. When they heard the sound and saw the torches, their worst fears were confirmed and they actually began killing one another in their panic.

It occurred to me recently that the devil has one tactic, and that tactic is fear. Why is that? It's because he lives in constant fear. It's what motivates him so therefore he uses fear because he knows it so well. Consider these encounters Jesus had with demons that revealed their terror: "In the synagogue there was a man possessed by a demon, an impure spirit. He cried out at the top of his voice, 'Go away! What do you want with us, Jesus of Nazareth? Have you come to destroy us? I know who you are—the Holy One of God!'" (Luke 4:33-34). Then again in Luke 8:38, "When he [the demon or legion of demons] saw Jesus, he cried out and fell at his feet, shouting at the top of his voice, 'What do you want with me, Jesus, Son of the Most High God? I beg you, don't torture me!'"

The way for Gideon to defeat his enemies was to be set free from his own fear so he could take advantage of his enemy's fear. The same is true for you. First John 4:18 tells us, "There is no fear in love. But perfect love drives out fear, because fear has to do with punishment. The one who fears is not made perfect in love." If you are fearful, it's not a lack of courage, it's a deficiency of love. As you grow in God's love and are free from fear, you are equipped to overcome the enemies of God who oppress His creation. Build yourself up in the love of God and fear cannot remain.

What are you operating in, fear or love? Where are you living a bold, fearless life? Where are you not living that kind of life? God knows how to set you free and to use your freedom to extend His kingdom where He sends you. I urge you this week to realize that fear is a tactic of the enemy from which God wants to set you free and then use your freedom to free others who are under the same bondage you once were in.

Week #11

Finding the More

Let's go back to a point I made concerning Gideon's thinking a few chapters ago (yes, I know I said we were moving on, but let's look at Gideon in this chapter for the last time—I promise). Gideon assumed he needed more if he was going to do what God was announcing. *More of what?* you ask. He thought he needed more of everything! He needed more courage, more confirmation that it was the Lord speaking to him, more soldiers for the army, more grace that God would not slay him on the spot for his recalcitrance. You can see that Gideon's thinking was the main obstacle preventing him from cooperating with God's plan. Until he changed his thinking, he was going to stay right where he was, doing what he had always done. The same is true for you.

In this chapter, let's look at this same tendency (to look for more) among Jesus' followers as we examine the time when Jesus fed the 5,000. This story is told in all four gospels, but I have chosen to use John's account in his gospel.

NEW THOUGHTS

Here is how John began his report:

> When Jesus looked up and saw a great crowd coming toward him, he said to Philip, "Where shall we buy bread for these people to eat?" He asked this only to test him, for he already had in mind what he was going to do. Philip answered him, "It would take more than half a year's wages to buy enough bread for each one to have a bite!" Another of his disciples, Andrew, Simon Peter's brother, spoke up, "Here is a boy with five small barley loaves and two small fish, but how far will they go among so many?" (John 6:5-8).

Jesus asked the question to reveal the limitation of His disciples' thoughts and faith at that point in time. Perhaps Jesus is asking you a question? If He is, you can be sure He already knows the answer, but in all probability you do not—which is why He is asking. On the one hand, Philip did a quick calculation of the cost to feed everyone and dismissed Jesus' idea since they needed more money. On the other hand, Andrew did an inventory of what they had on hand and concluded their stock was woefully short of what would be needed. Just like Gideon, Philip and Andrew assumed they needed *more* if and before they were going to act and perhaps thought Jesus was a little unrealistic to even consider such a possibility. Of course, Jesus was not the one with the problem. His disciples were in error, and this is still the same today.

Jesus asked the question and set up this scenario to give the disciples new ways of looking at their problems and challenges. He wanted them to see the situation as an *opportunity* but for them to see it the same way, they had to get rid of their small thinking and think bigger thoughts. Once again, the same is true for you and me.

WRONG AGAIN

You know the rest of the story of when Jesus fed the multitude, but just in case you don't remember, here it is:

> Jesus then took the loaves, gave thanks, and distributed to those who were seated as much as they wanted. He did the same with the fish. When they had all had enough to eat, he said to his disciples, "Gather the pieces that are left over. Let nothing be wasted." So they gathered them and filled twelve baskets with the pieces of the five barley loaves left over by those who had eaten (John 6:11-13).

Jesus did not need more money or more loaves and fish. He used what they had in their possession to feed the people. This process did not escape the notice of the crowd, who did some quick calculations of their own and concluded a great miracle had occurred. What did they do in response? Give thanks? Worship? Ask for prayer? No, they applied their limited thinking and decided to crown Jesus as their king:

> After the people saw the sign Jesus performed, they began to say, "Surely this is the Prophet who is to come into the world." Jesus, knowing that they intended to come and make him king by force, withdrew again to a mountain by himself (John 6:14-15).

What we see in this story is bad or wrong thinking on the front and back ends of the miracle, first on the part of the disciples and then of the crowd. The disciples should have known Jesus was teaching them a lesson and inquired, "What did You have in mind, Lord?" The crowd should have asked something like, "What does this mean for us, Lord? What is the lesson in what you just did?" They did not and Jesus had to make Himself scarce before they did something rash (of course, Jesus was already King, so it was another instance of wrong thinking on the people's part).

What about you? Is Jesus directing you to do something, but your thinking says, "I need more—more education, more time, more money, more knowledge"? Has Jesus done great things for you, but you are not extracting the correct lesson from His acts, and thus not applying those lessons to your purpose or creativity? You see, when Jesus does a great miracle, it's not so you can make *Him* more famous. It's so He can stimulate your faith that will take you to the next level of fruitfulness for Him.

This feeding miracle was not to highlight what *Jesus* could do; it showed what *His people* can do with Him in their midst. You don't need more; you only need Him—He is always enough. I encourage you to look at your life this week and see where you have been holding out for more before you act, now realizing that when you act, you will always find the more—in Him.

Week #12

Groundhog Day

In the movie, *Groundhog Day*, a weatherman played by actor Bill Murray wakes up on February 2, which is called Groundhog Day in the U.S., but then keeps awakening only to find himself living that same day again and again. Thus, the term "Groundhog Day" has come to mean an experience or event that tends to repeat itself in every detail.

There was actually an instance of this phenomenon in Jesus' ministry, and it involved the miracle we have come to know as the feeding of the multitude or the multiplication of the loaves and fishes. We looked at the first such miracle in the last chapter but remarkably the same miracle occurred shortly thereafter—but the disciples were oblivious to the similarities between the two scenarios. Let's look at the second miracle and see how it applies to our theme of unlocking the power of your thinking.

WRONG SIDE OF THE TRACKS

For the story of this second multiplication, let's look at Matthew's account:

> Jesus called his disciples to him and said, "I have compassion for these people; they have already been with me three days and have nothing to eat. I do not want to send them away hungry, or they may collapse on the way." His disciples answered, "Where could we get enough bread in this remote place to feed such a crowd?" "How many loaves do you have?" Jesus asked. "Seven," they replied, "and a few small fish." He told the crowd to sit down on the ground. Then he took the seven loaves and the fish, and when he had given thanks, he broke them and gave them to the disciples, and they

> in turn to the people. They all ate and were satisfied. Afterward the disciples picked up seven basketfuls of broken pieces that were left over. The number of those who ate was four thousand men, besides women and children (Matthew 15:32-38).

It's remarkable that the disciples saw no connection between this crowd and the one Jesus had previously fed. I would think one of them would have said, "Hey, this is just like before. Why don't we find out what we have, pray over it, and feed these people?" Not one of them did, however, and it was the groundhog-day principle in spiritual terms. From this, we can see that until they learned to change their thinking, they were destined, doomed even, to repeat the same behavior for the remainder of their days. The same is true for you.

There is a good chance the disciples did not think about feeding the crowd as they had previously done because of where this crowd was located. The first multiplication had taken place in Galilee among the Jews, but in Matthew 15, Jesus had taken them across the Lake to a region with more Gentiles. Perhaps they did not "think" God would or could bless those folks like He did their fellow Jews, so therefore it never occurred to them God wanted or was able to perform a similar miracle on that side of the Lake—which for them was on the wrong side of the tracks, so to speak.

HARDENING OF THE HEART-ERIES

In the next chapter, we will look at one more lesson from these two miracles pertaining to our thinking, but for now, let's see what we can learn to help us unlock the power of our own thinking. I suggest you start by identifying with these disciples in their situation. Pray, "Lord, I am just like Your followers in this story. My thinking is limited so therefore I easily forget what you have done in the past, and consequently miss opportunities to be part of what You want to do now."

Second, then pray, "God, open my eyes to where my thinking is limited or off due to a hardening of my heart-eries." Ask God to show you what you can't see because of your thinking where you, your purpose, or other people are concerned. Bad thinking not addressed can turn into a hardening of the heart, which you want to avoid. Once you have done this, then pray these words Paul wrote, but pray them for yourself:

> I pray that the eyes of *my* heart may be enlightened in order that *I* may know the hope to which *You* have called *me*, the riches of *Your* glorious inheritance in *Your* holy people, and *Your* incomparably great power for *me* who believes. That power is the same as the mighty strength *You* exerted when *You* raised Christ from the dead and seated him at *Your* right hand in the heavenly realms, far above all rule and authority, power and dominion, and every name that is invoked, not only in the present age but also in the one to come (Ephesians 1:18-21, pronouns in bold were changed by the author).

Pray this prayer over your life and work. Pray it again and again. Pray it with the intent to see where your thinking is deficient and thus limiting you just like it did the disciples at the second miraculous feeding. God has more for you than a groundhog-day life where you are restricted to each day's experience being pretty much the same as the previous day. There is no limit to what God can do with and for you *except* in your own mind and thinking. I encourage you to break out of the Groundhog Day mentality and cycle, freed to enjoy the exhilaration of God's ability to use you without the restrictions you have put on Him due to your limited thinking.

Week #13

A Sign

Let's examine once more the story of the feeding of the multitude to see what it can teach us about how to think. This time, we will examine the days following that miracle. We read that the leaders immediately came to Jesus to test Him:

> The Pharisees and Sadducees came to Jesus and tested him by asking him to show them a sign from heaven. He replied, "When evening comes, you say, 'It will be fair weather, for the sky is red,' and in the morning, 'Today it will be stormy, for the sky is red and overcast.' You know how to interpret the appearance of the sky, but you cannot interpret the signs of the times. A wicked and adulterous generation looks for a sign, but none will be given it except the sign of Jonah." Jesus then left them and went away (Matthew 16:1-4).

These are remarkable verses that tell us much. Let's get started.

A SIGN

Jesus had just fed a multitude with a few loaves and fish, but the Sadducees and Pharisees were not impressed. (By the way, those two parties or movements loathed one another, but here they came together to try and trick Jesus, asking Him for something they didn't believe He could produce.) You see, the Jews thought the devil could do signs on earth, which would include feeding a multitude, but they were asking for something more dramatic. They wanted to see the sun stand still or some other "sign from heaven." They were asking Jesus for an absolute and indisputable public demonstration of power. When you ask God for repeated confirmations of His will for your life, you may be doing the same, but I am getting ahead of myself.

Jesus basically responded by saying, "There are signs all around you, signs from heaven, and you don't know how to interpret them. Oh, you can predict the rain when you see God's creation acting in a certain way, but you are not able to figure out who I am and what I represent from those same signs." He then accused those leaders of being in bed, so to speak, with other gods by referring to them as "adulterous." It's not that they had abandoned their God; they had simply taken on mindsets and attitudes to supplement their worship of Jehovah. Later, James wrote that when we are friends with the world, we are also "adulterous" (see James 4:4).

Jesus promised His opponents a sign, but it would be the sign of Jonah, who was swallowed by a whale in which He spent three nights to think about God's will. Jesus was going to follow Jonah's example and "disappear" for three days, only to return to establish His kingdom and lead His followers to eternal life. When you pray for a sign to confirm God's will, you must remember that you have already received the sign of Jonah.

If you believe in the Resurrection, then you can believe God for anything—money, healing, ministry opportunities, your own business, or healing of relationships. After all, if God can raise the dead, He can any and all things and thus you have your sign that God is with you: "And if the Spirit of him who raised Jesus from the dead is living in you, he who raised Christ from the dead will also give life to your mortal bodies because of his Spirit who lives in you" (Romans 8:11).

"I'M DONE"

Then Matthew 16:4 reports something remarkable, a turning point in Jesus' ministry. Matthew wrote that "Jesus left them and went away." From that point on, Jesus was no longer trying to debate and woo the Pharisees and Sadducees. After this encounter, He said, "I'm done. You are stiff-necked and hard-hearted, and I'm withdrawing from you. With all the evidence, you have no interest in following Me or My ways. Even a sign from heaven would not cure your unbelief. By rejecting Me, you have rejected the Father."

It can be difficult to accept that Jesus was "done" with anyone and, of course, He did not withdraw completely. He was still present from time to time, but He spent most of His last days preparing His disciples rather than trying to argue and win over the leaders who had said in essence they were done with Jesus as well. Nothing He could have done would win their faith and loyalty, including coming back from the dead

The good news, as we will see in the next chapter, is that Jesus did take His disciples, went away, and began to prepare them more completely for what was to come. The good news for us is we are among that company with whom He still works to help us be on guard against the leaven or teaching of the Pharisees who are always around us. That teaching or leaven is really the thinking of the Pharisees to which we are all susceptible.

How about you? Are you asking God for a sign before you accept what's in your heart to do? Did you ever realize you have your sign, which was Jesus's Resurrection? It was His Resurrection that showed you the availability of God's power on your behalf. It was the Resurrection that eventually led to the outpouring of the Spirit who now lives in you to empower you to carry out God's will for your life. It was the Resurrection that positioned Jesus at the Father's right hand where He is praying and interceding for *you*.

You have the sign of Jonah and you don't need an unusual or unexpected manifestation so you can be sure you won't look foolish or fail as you step up and out in God's purpose for your life. Beware of the leaven of the Pharisees, which is the worldview that God owes you a full explanation and absolute confirmation before He expects you to take the steps of faith.

Week

#14

Mind Leaven

I need one more chapter to finish our look at the miracles called the feeding of the multitude or multiplication of the loaves and fishes. Our objective is to identify where and how our thinking has put limitations on God and ourselves as His servants. After Jesus had fed the crowd and the leaders confronted Him to demand a sign from heaven, we read this story:

> When they went across the lake, the disciples forgot to take bread. "Be careful," Jesus said to them. "Be on your guard against the yeast of the Pharisees and Sadducees." They discussed this among themselves and said, "It is because we didn't bring any bread. Aware of their discussion, Jesus asked, "You of little faith, why are you talking among yourselves about having no bread? Do you still not understand? Don't you remember the five loaves for the five thousand, and how many basketfuls you gathered? Or the seven loaves for the four thousand, and how many basketfuls you gathered? How is it you don't understand that I was not talking to you about bread? But be on your guard against the yeast of the Pharisees and Sadducees." Then they understood that he was not telling them to guard against the yeast used in bread, but against the teaching of the Pharisees and Sadducees (Matthew 16:5-12).

Let's unpack this passage to see what we can learn to help us in our study of the limitations our thinking can have where the things of God are concerned.

"WE FORGOT THE BREAD"

Jesus had just had another tense encounter with the Jews

and left them to get into the boat with His team. His mind was on the discussion with the crowd, so He warned the men to be careful and on guard against "the yeast" of their leaders. What is yeast? It is something small you introduce into bread dough that causes a reaction so the dough will rise or increase. Leaven is always negative when used in the Bible and often represents sin or an unhealthy influence. Jesus was warning His followers to avoid anything that could enter their being and minds and cause a negative reaction or lead to an ungodly conclusion. What was that in this case? It was the bad teaching or thinking of their leaders that demanded a sign from heaven.

Jesus' mind was on one topic, but unfortunately the disciples had their minds on something else: lunch. They had forgotten to bring bread so even though Jesus had just taken a little and fed thousands, they were preoccupied with what was important to them and not Him in the moment. Despite the fact that God Himself was speaking to them, they did not and could not comprehend what He was saying because they were distracted by their own thoughts. If that happened to them, I assure you it can happen to us.

Notice the difference between how Jesus responded to the leaders and how He responded to the men. He took His time to explain what He was trying to say after a gentle rebuke, while He played hide-and-seek with the leaders, refusing to give them a direct answer. That is good news for you and me, for we desperately need Jesus' insight and patience if we are going to unlock the power of our thinking by removing our preconceived notions of what we *think* we know or what we *think* He said.

CLARITY

The good news is God wants you to have clarity of thought and understanding where His will is concerned, but it's not always easy to obtain. For that to happen, you must surrender your infatuation with or absorption in three things:

1. **Your provision.** When God speaks to you, it's difficult not to jump to how questions: *How will this*

work out? How will I get paid? How exactly should I proceed? God will show you what to do but He has made one thing clear: He can and will provide for you regardless of where you are or what He asks you to do. Remember your past so you can have confidence today. He can multiply bread to feed you and your family, no matter how many are in it.

2. **Your future.** The disciples were concerned they would not have the provisions they needed for where they were headed. God will be on the other side of your lake no matter where He is taking you. See point number one and once again, remember your past.
3. **Your beliefs.** The fact that Jesus was warning them about teaching they had heard all their lives meant they had been infected with a spiritual virus that had impacted all their "files." It was important for them to examine what they believed, why they believed it, and do a virus scan, upgrade their software, and remove anything inconsistent with His teaching. I heard a pastor once recommend that we put our conclusions on a bulletin board and not in concrete, for then it is much easier to remove and replace them.

The last item may be the most difficult of all, for it requires you either unlearn what you heard that was not quite right or correct how you received what was right because you turned it into something it was not meant to be. For example, you could have heard a teaching point that you need to "give it to the Lord." You heard that but assumed it meant you must do nothing and God will do everything where your life situation is concerned. That was not bad advice, but you misapplied it and now must go back and unlearn and relearn what God meant when He said it.

I cannot emphasize strongly enough that if the disciples misunderstood Jesus when He was talking to them face to face, then you have misunderstood God even though the Spirit lives in you. That does not mean you are all wrong: far from it. It means God is with you, like He was with the men in the boat, to steer your thoughts to the right conclusion—but only if you allow Him to do so. The only thing required of you is that you submit your thoughts to Him and be open to adjustment, whether slight or drastic. If you will do that, you will have unlocked the power of your thinking because you refused to stubbornly hold on to any conclusion but joyfully submitted it to the Master's inspection for approval or correction.

Week

#15

Born Again Again

Let's move on from the stories of Jesus feeding the multitudes to Jesus' encounter with Nicodemus, the teacher of Israel. In this story, we learn that Nicodemus approached Jesus to hear the most recent word from a man of God. John reported,

> Now there was a Pharisee, a man named Nicodemus who was a member of the Jewish ruling council. He came to Jesus at night and said, "Rabbi, we know that you are a teacher who has come from God. For no one could perform the signs you are doing if God were not with him." Jesus replied, "Very truly I tell you, no one can see the kingdom of God unless they are born again." "How can someone be born when they are old?" Nicodemus asked. "Surely they cannot enter a second time into their mother's womb to be born!" Jesus answered, "Very truly I tell you, no one can enter the kingdom of God unless they are born of water and the Spirit. Flesh gives birth to flesh, but the Spirit gives birth to spirit. You should not be surprised at my saying, 'You must be born again.' The wind blows wherever it pleases. You hear its sound, but you cannot tell where it comes from or where it is going. So it is with everyone born of the Spirit" (John 3:1-7).

Let's look at some of the highlights of this story to see how they contribute to our theme of how to unlock the power of our thinking.

WHAT WE KNOW

Here are some things to consider about this story:

1. **Jesus was accessible.** We don't know how Nicodemus came to or found Him, but Jesus was willing to meet with him after His regular "office hours." All teachers and preachers should model their connection with the people after this because people need help connecting with or comprehending the messages and words they hear.
2. **Nicodemus did not ask any questions to start.** He simply came and affirmed that Jesus was a man from God. He had come perhaps to receive the latest word from the Lord to add to his own body of knowledge from which he taught.
3. **Nicodemus was *the* teacher in Israe**l. In verse 10, Jesus said, "You are Israel's teacher." In the Greek, there is a definite article before teacher, which should be translated, "You are *the* teacher of Israel." Nicodemus had a lot of experience and a reputation as a gifted teacher of the Law. He must have had a following and a reputation for Jesus to know who he was.
4. **After Jesus spoke, Nicodemus had a lot of *how* questions.** Jesus said he had to be born again of water and spirit and the great teacher responded with "how can? . . . he cannot? . . . can he? . . . how can?" (John 3:4, 9). When confronted with a teaching that did not fit his system, Nicodemus desperately looked for any way ***not*** to have to relearn what he had given his life to learn, apply, and teach.

Nicodemus was a Pharisee, a group that had over a period of 125 years of their existence as a movement made the Law a conglomeration of rules that were to be followed with external acts of righteousness. Jesus basically told him his system was worthless and incomplete without an encounter with the "church" who would eventually water baptize Jesus' followers and the Spirit who would lead and guide Jesus' followers.

THE LESSONS

What can we learn from this story to help us unlock the power of our thinking?

1. **You must often unlearn what you have previously learned**. An incomplete teaching or a good teaching you incompletely or incorrectly processed and filed will lodge in your brain and build a supporting cast of characters that will act to prevent you from getting to the whole truth. Nicodemus had to unlearn how he had processed the Law and relearn it in the power of the Spirit.
2. **You must be willing to unlearn and then relearn**. This requires a process of being born again and again where your mind is concerned. Over the years, I have had to re-evaluate my conclusions where women in ministry, giving, and the role of the Church are concerned. I had two choices: stubbornly maintain outdated, incomplete, or erroneous conclusions (asking like Nicodemus, 'how can this be?') or accept the fact that my original thinking needed to be "baptized" (drowned even) in Jesus' name and examined and restated by and through the Spirit. In order to be right, sometimes I had to admit I was wrong.
3. **You must be willing to take what you know to Jesus and allow Him to speak into it**. Be careful not to over-spiritualize this process. It requires you to do more than listen to a weekly sermon and read the latest fad book on some spiritual discipline. It means you are always on the hunt for renegade thoughts and attitudes that you need to corral and tame: ". . . we take captive every thought to make it obedient to Christ" (2 Corinthians 10:5b).

There is no easy way to take every thought captive except to become a child in your thinking again and again. You must constantly realize you are always the learner, never finished with the learning process. The good news is that God is with you as you do this because the Spirit lives in you. Where have you become like Nicodemus, confident in what you know and your reputation for that knowledge? Where are you confronted with positions and conclusions contrary to what you think? Is your response "How can I?" or "Speak, Lord, for Your servant listens"? If you want to unlock the power of your thinking, you will need to pay attention to where it may currently be locked into incomplete or stale thoughts so you can free it to think fresh new ones.

Week #16

Lunch Break

In this chapter, let's take a look at the story of the woman at the well in John 4 for our next lesson in how to unlock the power of your thinking. I'm going to skip over Jesus' discussion with the woman and go directly to the aftermath when His disciples returned with lunch. From there, we read

> Just then his disciples returned and were surprised to find him talking with a woman. But no one asked, "What do you want?" or "Why are you talking with her?" Then, leaving her water jar, the woman went back to the town and said to the people, "Come, see a man who told me everything I ever did. Could this be the Messiah?" They came out of the town and made their way toward him. Meanwhile his disciples urged him, "Rabbi, eat something." But he said to them, "I have food to eat that you know nothing about." Then his disciples said to each other, "Could someone have brought him food?" "My food," said Jesus, "is to do the will of him who sent me and to finish his work. Don't you have a saying, 'It's still four months until harvest'? I tell you, open your eyes and look at the fields! They are ripe for harvest. Even now the one who reaps draws a wage and harvests a crop for eternal life, so that the sower and the reaper may be glad together. Thus the saying 'One sows and another reaps' is true. I sent you to reap what you have not worked for. Others have done the hard work, and you have reaped the benefits of their labor" (John 4:27-38).

Let's take a closer look at this passage to see what we can learn.

SURPRISE, SURPRISE

When the disciples returned, they were in for a few surprises. The first was that Jesus was alone and speaking to a woman, a Samaritan woman no less—something rabbis had regularly taught should not be done with a Jewish woman let alone a hated Samaritan. John reported decades later when he wrote his gospel, "For Jews do not associate with Samaritans" (John 4:9b). Notice the present tense in that the Jews still wanted nothing to do with Samaritans years after Jesus was no longer on the scene. That's how deep their hatred and disdain were for that race of people. Perhaps their surprise was also that this woman would be interested in anything Jesus had to say—or that she could even comprehend it.

Then the disciples were surprised Jesus wasn't hungry. I would assume they went to get lunch because they were all hungry and in need of an afternoon pick-me-up, but there was Jesus, obviously enthused and no longer interested in the food they had purchased. By the way, I wonder where they were able to get food in the heart of Samaria that would meet their Jewish requirements? I would assume the Samaritans, who were part Jewish, kept kosher laws like they did but we don't know that for sure. Be that as it may, they had run their errand but Jesus seemed not to be hungry. He said He had food to eat they didn't know anything about and that was to do the will of His Father.

A BIGGER SURPRISE

I have often taught that an indication of your life purpose is to be able to do something and forget what time it is even if it's time to eat. If you can play the piano and realize, "Oh my, it's 3 p.m. and I missed lunch," then the piano has something to do with your purpose. Your purpose fulfills the statement that "man shall not live by bread alone; but man lives by every *word* that proceeds from the mouth of the LORD" (Deuteronomy 8:3b). Jesus' purpose was to "seek and save the lost" (Luke 19:10), so when He engaged this woman in His purpose, He was not as hungry as He had been when the disciples left. The same is true for you when you are in your purpose.

Yet, the disciples were in for an even bigger surprise, for their lunch break turned into a two-day revival:

> Many of the Samaritans from that town believed in him because of the woman's testimony, "He told me everything I ever did." So when the Samaritans came to him, they urged him to stay with them, and he stayed two days. And because of his words many more became believers (John 4:39-41).

Jesus and His entourage had left Judea after a heated exchange with the Pharisees and thought they were heading back to Galilee when an unexpected ministry opportunity opened for them in Samaria. Jesus had promised they would be fishers of men, but they assumed it would be in their homeland, not in the territory of their enemies. As if they had not had enough surprises for one day, Jesus told them they were about to reap a harvest from the seed He had planted in the woman's heart when many came out to see Him for themselves. Those men who went to fetch lunch were suddenly helping pull in a catch of souls for the Kingdom. When they returned, they had to change their thinking about food, Samaritans, the Kingdom, ministry, and what motivated and drove Jesus to do what He did.

That is the final point of this story. When you are in your purpose, God wants you to fulfill it more than you do. Just like Jesus did in this story, He goes ahead of you to prepare hearts and minds. You are harvesting purpose fruit for which you did not plant or water—Jesus did that on your behalf. He wants you to bear fruit in your purpose so He will promote and stir up interest in others for your presence. All you have to do is show up and reap the rewards, just like these men did in Samaria. If you want to unlock the power of your thinking where your purpose is concerned, then you must not think about what you could do and instead focus on how you can do what God has put right in front of you to do.

What can you do and forget to eat lunch? Where does the joy of the Lord overpower your physical needs and give you energy to perform and produce? Where is it that when you show up, good things happen for and to you? Where do you get the sense you are enjoying the fruits of someone else's labor? That's due to nothing you have done; it's simply the harvest due to the seed Jesus has sown in the minds and hearts of your "audience." Just be prepared to constantly be surprised at what you can do in Him or rather what He will do for you (and where He will do it) that will bring you purpose success.

Week #17

Thought Missionaries

Recently during a video recording for my website, I was talking about how important it is to get in touch with your heart and not just your head or intellect if you are going to discover your purpose. It is the heart where God writes His commandments. It is the heart where the Spirit of God communicates with His children. It is the heart that fuels the mouth as Jesus informed us: "For the mouth speaks what the heart is full of" (Luke 6:45b). This is a perfect introduction to this chapter, which focuses on the story of when Jesus instructed His disciples about forgiveness in Matthew 18. Let's go there now.

HOW MANY TIMES?

In Matthew 18, Jesus taught His followers how to confront sin in the church: If a person sins, go to them, and if they don't listen, take a delegation, and so forth. It is interesting Peter rightly concluded Jesus was not only addressing church discipline but forgiveness, for he asked the Lord a short time after His teaching, "Lord, how many times shall I forgive my brother or sister who sins against me? Up to seven times?" (Matthew 18:21). It seems Peter was coming to the Lord expecting some kind of commendation for his question since in his mind he was proving he had figured out how to do what Jesus had taught them to do.

Why would Peter have asked what he did, assuming he would win Jesus' approval and affirmation? It is because the rabbinical teaching of the day was there was to be ***no*** forgiveness extended for a third offense. Peter, therefore, was showing Jesus how far he was willing to go with His teaching, forgiving three-and-a-half times more than the rabbis had suggested. In modern terminology, Jesus then "blew Peter's mind" by putting a damper on Peter's show of magnanimity, "I tell you, not seven times, but seventy-seven times" (Matthew 18:22). Let's take a quick look into Peter's mind to see what we can learn to help us unlock the power of our thinking.

UNLEARNING

Peter had probably heard for most of his life, "Forgive once, forgive twice, but no more." He thought about it and that "truth" had taken root, so to speak, in his mind. Think of that teaching as a thought missionary. The concept took up residence and began to build a community of thoughts around it, just like a missionary who goes to another culture to make or teach converts. Eventually that forgive-twice thought built a village and then eventually a town and a city of similar, supportive thoughts.

Therefore, when Peter heard Jesus' teaching, he was looking for a way to add His teaching as a friendly neighbor to his existing cluster of forgiveness thoughts. However, Jesus would not allow Peter to do that and closed out his teaching by taking Peter out of his head and into his heart: "This is how my heavenly Father will treat each of you unless you forgive your brother or sister from your heart" (Matthew 18:35). In this case, Peter needed a new heart thought that would become another thought missionary, going into Peter's mind to displace the old thoughts about limited forgiveness. That new thought would then need time to create their own village of supportive thoughts to help apply and live out Jesus' teaching.

In other words, Peter had to unlearn what he had learned and with the help of his heart, re-educate his mind to think anew. He needed to send new thought missionaries that did not make sense based on what he had been taught but would in time equip Peter to express and flow in Jesus' new directives. You are in need of the same thing. When you read, "Be generous," if you don't unlearn what you think you know about generosity, you will do what Peter did. You will go to the Lord with the new "percentage" level of your giving, thinking you are being magnanimous, only to hear the Lord say, "I don't want 10%, I want it all!"

If you don't unlearn your assumption that you are too young or too old to do God's will, your mind will also be blown when the Spirit says to you, "I want you to go here or there *now*." If you don't send some new thought missionaries to convert your old thoughts when you read Jesus commands you to forgive your enemies who hurt you, you will say, "No way!"

Are your heart and mind working together to renew and re-educate your mind? Are you sending thought missionaries in the power of the Spirit from your heart to your head? Are you willing to have your mind blown with new thoughts that can then take up residence and ease out the old to create a new colony of beliefs that will lead to new actions? I hope you are for there is no other way but to unlearn and then relearn what you need in order to be transformed into a new creature conformed to the image of Christ.

Week #18

With God

In our quest to unlock the power of our thinking, we have seen on several occasions how Jesus acted and then taught the disciples, constantly confronting their limited or misapplied thinking and assumptions. The disciples saw Jesus talking with a Samaritan woman, heard him warn against the teaching of the Pharisees, and witnessed Him feed a multitude with a few scraps of food on two occasions. In each instance, the men struggled to wrap their minds around what Jesus was doing and saying not because they were rebellious or obstinate but because the thoughts they had were inadequate to process the events they saw.

In other words, they needed new thoughts if they were going to apply what they saw and heard, which Jesus was glad to provide. In this chapter, let's examine another story which took the followers to new places in their minds and that is Jesus' encounter with the rich young ruler in Mark 10:17-31. You may wish to read those verses before you move on.

WHO THEN?

When Jesus told the young man to sell what he owned and follow Him, the man who knelt before Jesus was crestfallen: "At this the man's face fell. He went away sad, because he had great wealth" (Mark 10:22). Jesus then gave a commentary on what had just happened: "Jesus looked around and said to his disciples, 'How hard it is for the rich to enter the kingdom of God!'" (Mark 10:23). Once again, the disciples were dumbfounded: "The disciples were amazed at his words" (Mark 10:24a) only to have Jesus drive the point home even more emphatically:

> "Children, how hard it is to enter the kingdom of God!
> It is easier for a camel to go through the eye of a needle

> than for someone who is rich to enter the kingdom of God" (Mark 10:24-b-25).

His words had their usual effect: "The disciples were even more amazed, and said to each other, 'Who then can be saved?'" (Mark 10:26).

It's interesting the disciples did not direct their question to the Lord Himself, but it didn't matter. He went on to give them even further explanation of the incident with the young ruler and what it represented. It was prevalent among the Jews that God favored those who were rich because they had kept the Law. The young ruler wasn't so sure of that, so he came to receive confirmation and consolation from Jesus who shattered their pretense that wealth was a sure sign of God's blessing. The disciples shared in the young man's dismay and were amazed, asking "Who then?" could be saved if the rich of all people could not.

THE REST OF THE STORY

Jesus answered their question with a new thought for them to consider, a thought missionary that would take root and grow in their minds to replace their old thought process: "Jesus looked at them and said, 'With man this is impossible, but not with God; all things are possible with God.'" There are two ways to interpret this. One is that God can save the rich regardless of the obstacles and, in a sense, that is certainly correct. Yet there is a more subtle but appropriate message beyond God's ability to save that rich man or any rich person.

What Jesus said is not a statement proving all things are possible with God. *Rather it is a statement that nothing is impossible for a person who walks and works with God.* The first interpretation puts all the emphasis and responsibility on God; the second states that people have a role in walking out their obedience in partnership with God.

Jesus told the young ruler, "If you will follow me, you will be able to gain the eternal life you seek. I will walk with you and help you do what seems impossible for you to do!" That truth is consistent not only for salvation and eternal life, but also for carrying out your purpose and creativity along the way. You cannot expect God to do what only you can do, but when you do what you can do, God will walk with you. If you go and walk with God, *all* things are possible.

What are you putting off because, in your mind, God has to do it? I urge you to adjust your thinking to see that God will indeed do it but *only* if *you* do something first. You are His agent who must go and carry Him with you wherever go, whether into your workshop, studio, office, classroom, family, or church. You need more action thoughts and less passive ones if you are going to do the impossible, not only dreaming about great things but achieving them—with Him.

That is the only way to enter the Kingdom, which was actually the issue at stake when the young man asked his question. May you be bold to draw on the power of God so you can do the things God has put in your heart to do to extend His kingdom in which you have been made a citizen and partner.

Week #19

Dull Thinking

The last few chapters have focused on Jesus' attempts to help His disciples have new thoughts that would enable them (and us) to unlock the power of their thinking. Now let's move on to Matthew 15 to examine another encounter between Jesus and the Pharisees, whose thinking was distorted by tradition and assumptions of what God wanted in various situations. As you read on, don't look to add to your already negative view of the Pharisees but with an eye to determine if you are like they were in this story.

WASHED UP

The Pharisees approached the finest teacher of their day who was impacting the entire nation to ask Him a question. Did they choose to ask something important that would contribute to a deeper understanding of God? They did not, but instead wanted to know why He didn't wash His hands:

> Then some Pharisees and teachers of the law came to Jesus from Jerusalem and asked, "Why do your disciples break the tradition of the elders? They don't wash their hands before they eat!" (Matthew 15:1-2).

When the Pharisees washed, they scrubbed carefully all the way up to their elbows, but they never observed Jesus doing the same. Therefore, they approached the King of the universe to talk about their tradition of how far up their arm one should cleanse before eating. That is the power tradition has not only on your thinking but also on your ability to discern God's priorities. You eventually assume your tradition is what God wants and should be observed by *everyone*.

Jesus summarized what they had done by saying, "Thus you

nullify the word of God for the sake of your tradition" (15:6b). Jesus then turned to the crowd and delivered a short teaching: "Listen and understand. What goes into someone's mouth does not defile them, but what comes out of their mouth, that is what defiles them" (15:10-11). His words had the double effect of teaching the people and rebuking the Pharisees, who were increasingly becoming "washed up" and irrelevant to God and the people because of their meaningless traditions.

"YOU DON'T GET IT"

The disciples came to Jesus and inquired, "Do you know that the Pharisees were offended when they heard this?" (15:12). Jesus then gave them some advice that you would be wise to follow as well: "Leave them; they are blind guides. If the blind lead the blind, both will fall into a pit" (15:14). Jesus essentially told them to stop paying attention to the voice of tradition and listen to Him. At this point, I'm sure you are thinking if not saying aloud, "Yes, that's right. Listen to the voice of God!" Before you get too smug in your appraisal, however, look a little further:

> Peter said, "Explain the parable to us." "Are you still so dull?" Jesus asked them. "Don't you see that whatever enters the mouth goes into the stomach and then out of the body? But the things that come out of a person's mouth come from the heart, and these defile them" (15:16-18).

The disciples did not get the real message because they were as steeped in tradition as the Pharisees. They didn't get what Jesus was saying so He went on to explain that He wasn't referring to hand washing or foods to eat (or not) but the condition of the heart. What did Jesus do next? He took the men on a field trip to demonstrate His lesson, just like He is trying to do for you:

> Leaving that place, Jesus withdrew to the region of Tyre and Sidon. A Canaanite woman from that vicinity came to him, crying out, "Lord, Son of David, have mercy on me! My daughter is demon-possessed and suffering terribly" (15:21-22).

After hearing her request, Jesus said, "It is not right to take the children's bread and toss it to the dogs" (15:26). Isn't it interesting that Matthew connected this story in his gospel narrative to the hand washing, heart-condition lesson Jesus had just taught? He did so to clearly show them the correct understanding of His teaching.

When Jesus spoke to this woman in what seemed to be such a harsh way, He was mirroring for the men their own heart attitude toward women, Gentiles, and people in need. They heard it, saw it, and saw Jesus' response healing the woman's daughter, but still didn't get it. How do I know this? I know because in Acts 10:13-15, a vision of a sheet came to Peter:

> Then a voice told him, "Get up, Peter. Kill and eat." Surely not, Lord!" Peter replied. "I have never eaten anything impure or unclean." The voice spoke to him a second time, "Do not call anything impure that God has made clean."

Peter had heard Jesus' teaching in Matthew 15 but a few years later he was still clinging to his kosher ways while also considering Gentiles unclean. Just like in Matthew 15 when Jesus took the men to the encounter with the Syro-Phoenician woman, after his sheet vision Jesus took Peter to the home of the Roman centurion Cornelius. Even though Jesus had spoken to Peter and taught him face to face, he still didn't get it. There is a good chance we are in the same condition.

Where is your tradition, whether it be what you do or believe keeping you from hearing and doing the will of God? Where have you assumed your tradition is the absolute will of God for *all* people, not just you? Where is your thinking dull like Peter's was? Where is your prejudice keeping you from seeing others as God sees them? From seeing yourself as God sees you?

If you are going to unlock the power of your thinking, you have to ruthlessly examine your thoughts and jettison any you got from a bad teaching or the result of the erroneous way you processed a good teaching. Hearing from the Lord is not enough, as the accounts in Matthew 15 show us. We must hear and then examine all our thoughts and ways in light of what we've learned to determine if we are walking in a way pleasing to the Lord or in the way of tradition.

Week #20

Locked On

Romans 12:2 states, "Do not conform to the pattern of this world but be transformed by the renewing of your mind. Then you will be able to test and approve what God's will is—his good, pleasing and perfect will." Since the business of the mind is thinking, then to experience the transformation we often seek and desperately need, we must think new thoughts, confronting current ones to see where they prevent or limit us from doing God's will. In this chapter, let's look at some thinking on the part of the Jews that caused them to misinterpret what Jesus did in Mark 3 because they locked on to the thought "God would never do that" and thus locked out other possibilities. Let's get started.

HEALING ON THE SABBATH

In Mark 2, Jesus had just violated the Sabbath, or so the Pharisees thought, when He and His disciples had picked and eaten some heads of grain. Then Mark reported another Sabbath incident immediately following:

> Another time Jesus went into the synagogue, and a man with a shriveled hand was there. Some of them were looking for a reason to accuse Jesus, so they watched him closely to see if he would heal him on the Sabbath. Jesus said to the man with the shriveled hand, "Stand up in front of everyone." Then Jesus asked them, "Which is lawful on the Sabbath: to do good or to do evil, to save life or to kill?" But they remained silent. He looked around at them in anger and, deeply distressed at their stubborn hearts, said to the man, "Stretch out your hand." He stretched it out, and his hand was completely restored. Then the Pharisees went out and began

to plot with the Herodians how they might kill Jesus (Mark 3:1-6).

Jesus did not lead the man with the shriveled hand out the back door of the synagogue to heal him, nor did He request that the man come back on Sunday or Monday. When Jesus asked the observers a question, they remained silent, which angered Jesus because He knew what their silence meant. Therefore, He openly challenged the onlookers' interpretation of Sabbath regulations by healing the man right in front of everyone.

Today, we are a bit taken aback by the response of the people who were in "church" that day. They did not run home to summon a close relative who had a similar condition. They did not request that Jesus not heal on the Sabbath, but instead come back on Tuesday when they could assemble others who needed a physical touch. They did not shake the man's restored hand and rejoice in his restoration. Instead, they had a quick confab to process and discuss what had just happened and agreed that "Jesus must die!" What's more, they conspired with the Herodians, those who supported the presence of the hated Romans through their puppet king Herod and put out a contract on Jesus' life.

GOD WOULD NEVER . . .

This story reveals an approach to the Sabbath that stipulated little to nothing was to be done on that day for fear of alienating and offending God—a noble thought. Yet once they locked on to their rigid interpretation, they locked out any other possibility. When Jesus healed a man right in front of their eyes by restoring a dysfunctional limb, the crowd did not see and could not appreciate what had occurred. Their thought was "God would never heal on the Sabbath" and thus they concluded Jesus was a Sabbath-breaker deserving of capital punishment.

Yet the stories in the gospels are not just an historical account for our entertainment. They are stories with lessons for our own lives, for we are just as susceptible to the thinking of the Jews who were in the synagogue. We can lock on to our thoughts and conclusions and lock out any other possibility, thus opposing instead of appreciating what God is teaching us. For example, you may hold on to a job you hate or where you are mistreated because you think, "I need this job; I've had this job 20 years and get an extra week's vacation next year." Thus, God's attempts to move you to something better are to no avail. Why? Because of your thinking.

Your thoughts about yourself or your abilities can also thwart God's desire to use you because you demean or diminish the effect you could have on others due to your stubborn resistance to a limited or skewed perspective of who you are in Him. You have been told you're a good artist, but you have locked on to the fact that you are not. You would like to travel and do missions work, but you have convinced yourself you don't travel well or are too poor to do so—locking on to your lack instead of your Source. Like the Jews, you think "God would never—fund my trip, or use me in that way, or use my creativity to bless and minister to others."

Where have you seen God move in your life or the lives of others yet you conspire with others to stay right where you are (listening to your friends tell you how that 'can't be God') so you can keep doing what you have always done? Where has your doctrine, which is nothing more than what you think about God and His will, actually limited or frustrated God's purpose for you? How have you taken what you hear and worked it in your mind to conclude "God would never do or want that—in my life or the lives of others"? These are difficult questions to ask, and the potential answers can be painful to face, but you must learn to confront and change your own thoughts and conclusions if you are to continue to grow in the wisdom and knowledge of God for your life.

Week #21

The Beauty of Holiness

In this chapter, let's consider a verse from Psalm 96:9: "Worship the Lord in holy array" (NASB). The King James Version states the same verse, "O worship the Lord in the beauty of holiness." The King James seems to place the label of holiness on the Lord (or perhaps that is simply how I choose to read it) but instead, let's assume the adjective of holiness belongs on the worshiper, not the One being worshiped. What are the implications for the perspective that the status of holiness is conferred on us as we worship the Lord?

HOLINESS

There is an aspect of holiness that has little to do with avoiding sin. It doesn't speak to the state of sinlessness in which you do not watch bad movies or utter profanity. It doesn't pertain to praying and reading the Bible. Instead, it's more about the fact that when you're holy, you're set apart for a special service or expression. For example, my mother had special dishes she only used when company came. Those dishes were set apart, and therefore were holy to her because they had a special use. You are holy in the same sense that God has set you apart to do something only you can do, to be something only you can be.

What's more, you are set apart due to the fact that there is, and there never has been or will be again, anyone like you. You have a set of fingerprints and a DNA code that have never existed. They are not recycled from someone who existed 100 years ago. You are holy unto the Lord, a unique creation with a distinct personality, gift mix, and way of processing sensory input. So far, you may be thinking, *That's great, but what has this got to do with unlocking my thinking?* The most important impact this fact can have on you is in how you view and think about *yourself*, which will in turn influence what you do with your purpose and gifts God has bestowed on you.

INDIVIDUALITY

If and when you are biased against yourself, you may attempt to become like others or simply attempt to distort who you are. Yet "who you are" is an important part of your creativity and purpose, for you must inject and invest who you are into what you do for it to be all God intends it to be. For example, the writers of the four gospels injected who they were into their accounts. They used their vocabulary, style of writing, experience, heritage, unique insights, and relationships (Mark was Peter's assistant) to flavor their gospel accounts. They did not all write the same way using the same format or approach. They were unique and thus each gospel was unique, or should I say it was holy—set apart for a specific purpose.

Examples would also abound throughout the world of creativity. A master painter had a unique style and forgeries can come close but cannot exactly replicate what is being copied because those copying cannot capture the essence of who the artist was. The same would be true for writers, sculptors, preachers, teachers, athletes, coaches, and any other expression of life and work. You have been set apart for a work only you can produce and that means you must be *you* to produce it. You can emulate someone else, but even when doing that you will involve your unique interpretation of what you are emulating. It will still be yours but will never be mistaken for the one you are modeling—even though it's close.

This means you can stop thinking about being someone else even when you are trying to be like someone else, for you will be like them as only *you* can be and do. Therefore, you don't have to fear being yourself as you express your purpose and creativity. In fact, you have a mandate to do so as only you can do. As you serve the Lord in the beauty of your holiness as a unique expression of God's creation, you will then truly worship Him because you will confess that since you are good enough for God, you are also good enough for yourself.

Week #22

"Spare Yourself, Lord"

Many of our lessons so far have come from Jesus' encounters with His disciples as He confronted and corrected their incomplete or erroneous thoughts, replacing them with new ways to think and act. In this chapter, let's look at another instance of Jesus with His disciples, this time involving Peter in their well-known discussion that shocks us each time we read it.

THE RESPONSE

In Matthew 16, Jesus had taken His disciples far north of Galilee where they could spend some alone time without the crowds or spies sent from Jerusalem. While there, He asked them who He was in the eyes of the public but then asked them who *they* thought He was. Peter then gave His answer based on the Father's revelation that Jesus was "the Messiah, the Son of the living God" (Matthew 16:16). Jesus ordered the men not to tell anyone what Peter had just told them, and went on to the next level of their training so He could prepare them for what was ahead:

> "From that time on Jesus began to explain to his disciples that he must go to Jerusalem and suffer many things at the hands of the elders, the chief priests and the teachers of the law, and that he must be killed and on the third day be raised to life" (Matthew 16:21).

When Peter heard this, He was concerned for his Messiah, himself, and their mission together so he pulled Jesus aside and said, "Never, Lord! This shall never happen to you!" (Matthew 16:22), to which Jesus gave His stunning reply, "Get behind me, Satan! You are a stumbling block to me; you do not have in mind the concerns of God, but merely human concerns" (Matthew 16:22).

Peter thought he was protecting Jesus, in essence saying, "Spare yourself, Lord. You don't have to do or go through that ordeal. You're better than that." Yet in his ignorance, Peter had unwittingly become a spokesman for Satan which Jesus recognized right away. If the story had ended there, we would not have the complete picture, one that gives us lessons to apply today as we seek to unlock the power of our own thinking.

THE REST OF THE STORY

Jesus turned to all the disciples after He rebuked Peter and continued,

> "Whoever wants to be my disciple must deny themselves and take up their cross and follow me. For whoever wants to save their life will lose it, but whoever loses their life for me will find it. What good will it be for someone to gain the whole world, yet forfeit their soul? Or what can anyone give in exchange for their soul? For the Son of Man is going to come in his Father's glory with his angels, and then he will reward each person according to what they have done" (Matthew 16:24-27).

There can be no new thinking unless the power and concept of the cross are part of the foundation. Peter was protecting himself as well as Jesus when he said what he did, but Jesus explained there can be no success in carrying out the will of God without denying self, taking up a cross, and following Jesus. In my own life, the cross has manifested in many ways. We moved 11 times in 33 years to follow what we believed was God's will. I turned down admission to Harvard and Carnegie Mellon Universities to pursue ministry.

I have suffered at the hands of church people for 47 years (sometimes through my own failures, other times at the hands of mean-spirited people and leaders). I have had to sit in silence when others were teaching things and had little idea what they were saying. One time when I was a pastor, I opened our refrigerator and all we had in it was a bottle of water and a box of corn flakes in the cupboard.

Today, I flow in purpose and creativity, but it wasn't always like this. I tried to spare myself the agony of some of the death-to-self experiences (and there are plenty more I did not mention) but to no avail. I'm still trying to learn how to do what Paul wrote in Colossians 3:2: "Set your minds on things above, not on earthly things." How about you? Where are you avoiding the cross? Where is how to deny self not prevalent in your plans?

Remember, Peter went from divine revelation to divine consternation in a matter of minutes, so your past revelation is no guarantee your current thinking is sanctified and correct. The only way you can ensure it is unlocked is to lock on to the truth that if you want to find your life, you will not be able to spare yourself from the tough times. You are going to have to lose your life along the way and trust that it will find you again no matter where you are or what you are doing.

Week #23

As a Man Thinketh

I have not drawn much from the Old Testament in this series, but let's change that in this chapter by looking at one of the best-known and oft-quoted verses pertaining to one's thought life. It's found in Proverbs 23:7 and for our purposes, let's look at it in its context:

> Do not eat the bread of a miser, nor desire his delicacies; *for as he thinks in his heart, so is he.* "Eat and drink!" he says to you, but his heart is not with you. The morsel you have eaten, you will vomit up, and waste your pleasant words (Proverbs 23:6-8 NKJV, emphasis added).

What can we learn about this verse and why Solomon penned it?

CONTEXT

I have used this verse to corroborate the truth of what Jesus said, "But those things which proceed out of the mouth come from the heart, and they defile a man" (Matthew 15:18). Yet Proverbs 23:7 is *not* addressing the issues of the heart-and-mouth connection. It was addressing a man who appears to be generous and welcoming, but in reality is not. He's what's known as a *miser* so he is actually counting the cost of what he is giving others while pretending to be generous. He knows the value of what he's giving away and it's troubling him to share so much with anyone who partakes of what he has.

I had a friend who used to say, "People know the price of things but seldom consider the value of them." He used it when we would offer a seminar that had a registration fee. There were people who only looked at the price but did not consider that they could receive great value from the seminar material. It was interesting that those same people would often complain because their companies would not invest in them, but they would turn around and do exactly what their company was doing—not invest in themselves.

Instead of making the miser in Proverbs 23:7 someone else, let's examine it from the point of view that we—you and I—are that miser. If that's true, how would being like him impact our thinking and how could we then unlock that area to find new power in our thoughts?

IT'S HIS MONEY

When I was a church administrator, I encountered many miserly people. We would pay whatever the utility company said to pay but we refused to bless a staff member with a $50 gift certificate. When working with those people, I would often say, "It's not my money, it's the Lord's." When most people heard that, they assumed I meant what is usually intended: "We are frugal because God has given us this money and we are going to be careful, *very* careful, how we spend it." That was not what I meant at all.

My intended sense was this: "This is the Lord's money. What do I care if He wants us to give it to missionaries, someone on our staff, someone in the church who has a need, or for something that would make life easier for our staff? If it's His money and if He has plenty more where that came from as we claim, then why should we be tightfisted with it?"

You see, some of us feign generosity, but we are nervous like the miserly person in Proverbs 23. We are concerned others are consuming what we want to hold on to, what we believe is ours to own. What's more, it's not about money really, it's blocking or preventing the testimony or gifts we could produce because it's going to cost us something—just like the miser. Jesus said, "Heal the sick, raise the dead, cleanse those who have leprosy, drive out demons. Freely you have received; freely give." (Matthew 10:8). What if that last phrase became your byline or motto for living? How would "freely received, freely give" change your thinking from where it is now? You would probably give more of yourself and that may or may not include money. Just as I said, "It's the Lord's money," it's also His testimony, His gift, His creativity, and His life you possess, not to own but to steward.

The problem with the phrase "as a man thinketh" is that it is potentially true for *all* of us, not just those we don't like or who don't do like we want them to. It is necessary for me to seek the Lord and inquire, "Where am I acting one way that makes people think I am in line with Your will, but in reality, I'm counting the cost and I don't like that it's costing me so much? Where am I being a miser with those around me which is of no benefit to them or me?"

Move across the table this week from the seat of the one eating with the miser and look at yourself as being the miser. Are you serving others a banquet of who you are and what you have, or are you pretending to do that a few hours a week, while secretly stashing away the best of who you are for your own consumption? If that's the case, then it's time to remind yourself that "it's not your money or life" and start thinking of how you can spend it and spread it around.

Week #24

A Kingdom Mind

Let's return to the New Testament where we once again find Jesus addressing His disciples' thinking. We read in Acts 1:3-6,

> During the forty days after he suffered and died, he appeared to the apostles from time to time, and he proved to them in many ways that he was actually alive. And he talked to them about the Kingdom of God. Once when he was eating with them, he commanded them, "Do not leave Jerusalem until the Father sends you the gift he promised, as I told you before. John baptized with water, but in just a few days you will be baptized with the Holy Spirit." So when the apostles were with Jesus, they kept asking him, "Lord, has the time come for you to free Israel and restore our kingdom?" (NLT).

We first see Jesus proclaiming the Kingdom in Matthew 4:17: "Repent of your sins and turn to God, for the Kingdom of Heaven is near." As He prepared to depart in Acts, He was still teaching and talking about the Kingdom. Yet it seems that the disciples didn't quite "get" it, for we see them asking, "Has the time come for you to free Israel and restore the kingdom?" Jesus answered them by directing them back to His promise: "But you will receive power when the Holy Spirit comes upon you. And you will be my witnesses, telling people about me everywhere" (Acts 1:8). The Spirit was the key to unlock their thinking and He is the key for us as well. Let's examine what that means to see what lessons we can learn.

THE MIND SET ON THE SPIRIT

Paul wrote these words to the Romans:

> Those who are dominated by the sinful nature think about sinful things, but those who are controlled by the Holy Spirit think about things that please the Spirit. So letting your sinful nature control your mind leads to death. But letting the Spirit control your mind leads to life and peace. For the sinful nature is always hostile to God. It never did obey God's laws, and it never will. That's why those who are still under the control of their sinful nature can never please God (Romans 8:5-8, NLT).

Paul indicated "letting the Spirit control your mind" produces life and peace. What does it mean for the Spirit to control your mind? Are we simply radio towers that receive and then file away or broadcast heavenly spiritual thoughts? Is it a description of the familiar scene in movies where the devil is perched on one shoulder whispering into our ear while God is on the other shoulder doing the same? Do all our thoughts have their origin in one spiritual source or the other?

Let's go back to Acts 1. Those men had been with Jesus for more than three years and they had just experienced a 40-day post-Resurrection crash course and overview of Jesus' Kingdom teaching. Yet they still did not understand for they asked Him a political question about when Israel would be freed from Rome's control. When the Spirit was poured out in Acts 2, *then* they understood it all and could share it with power to interested listeners.

KINGDOM-MINDED

When the Spirit came, the disciples had the power and a new intellectual capacity to comprehend what Jesus had taught and shown them. Peter's sermon in Acts 2 explained Jesus, exalted Jesus, taught Jesus, demonstrated Jesus. The sermon clearly outlined that Jesus was the King of the Kingdom: "So let everyone in Israel know for certain that God has made this Jesus, whom you crucified, to be both Lord and Messiah!" (Acts 2:36). They did not preach against Rome, lay out a new Law, or preach holiness. The Spirit focused their thoughts and minds on Jesus.

What does this teach us? It teaches that the Spirit does not wish to control every thought, but to impart a new operating system that is Kingdom-minded which is all about Jesus—not about Jesus and politics, or Jesus and my career, or Jesus and my investments. There cannot be Jesus and *anything* else. It is only about Jesus. That was why the disciples had to wait for the Spirit. Otherwise, their presentation would have lacked proper focus. It's easy to say it's all about Jesus, but Jesus knew better. That's why He told His disciples they would have to deny themselves, pick up their cross, and follow Him. That was what the Kingdom was all about.

What is on your mind? Is it how lonely you are? Are you asking why you aren't married or why you don't have a better job? I'm not demeaning your loneliness or your poverty, but the Spirit comes to give you the mind of Christ about Christ and what that means for your daily life. Thoughts controlled by the sinful nature are "self" thoughts, while thoughts of the Spirit are about Jesus and His purpose and plan for your life that may or may not include spouse, children, Wall Street riches, or living where you want to live.

The Kingdom has a King and He is supreme—or "Lord of all" to put it in biblical terms. I urge you to invite the Spirit into your mind not to control your every thought, but to impart the proper foundation for the Kingdom enabling you to evaluate your thoughts more effectively. When you do that, your old nature will no longer control your mind and you will be free to think the thoughts of God that will direct you where to work, what to do, and how to be a person of purpose.

Week #25

You-Turn

Let's stay in the New Testament but move on to Revelation. You may think that's an unusual place to go to talk about thinking, and I thought the same when I had the idea. I believe it's God's leading, however, but you be the judge as we proceed to Revelation chapter two.

REPENT

After a brief introduction in Revelation, Jesus evaluated seven churches giving them specific feedback concerning the reality of their spiritual condition. He commended some but rebuked others, ending all seven messages with the same phrase, "Whoever has ears, let them hear what the Spirit says to the churches. To the one who is victorious . . ." He then gave a specific promise for those who heard and were victorious. We will examine those promises in the next few chapters, but for now, let's look at His comments to the Ephesian church: "Consider how far you have fallen! Repent and do the things you did at first. If you do not repent, I will come to you and remove your lampstand from its place" (Revelation 2:5). Let's look at the word or command used twice in that verse and that word is *repent*.

When you hear the word *repent*, what are your thoughts? For some, it represents contrition or sorrow for sin and if that is what you think, you are not wrong. Yet the literal meaning of the Greek word for repent *metanoia* is "to change one's mind or attitude about." What happens when you change your mind? It means you think differently about something. Another definition of repent is to "turn and go in another direction." So when you change your mind about something, it should impact your behavior and take you in a new direction. God told the Ephesians to repent and do the things they did at first. Their change of mind was to impact their behavior and deeds. In essence, Jesus advised them to make a U-turn and walk a different path.

EARS TO HEAR

For the Ephesian church, having "ears that hear" seems to have been connected to their willingness to repent. If they were not willing to address their thoughts, their ears would be closed and they would not inherit the promise, which for them was "I will give the right to eat from the tree of life, which is in the paradise of God" (Revelation 2:7). When we don't repent, we too become hard of hearing and we forfeit the benefits of the tree of life as it was portrayed in Genesis. When that happens, God does not direct our work as He did in the Garden. Instead, we pick and choose what we will do and how we will do it. We may be faithful but we are not flexible, and therefore only move in one direction. It could be referred to as our routine which can turn into a rut—and someone said a rut is a grave with the ends extended.

Jesus had warned His disciples long before Revelation was written that they needed to be careful how they listened and heard. We read in Luke 8:8, "Whoever has ears to hear, let them hear." That warning came at the end of the parable of the sower, which taught that unless we adjust our heart condition, we will not be able to receive the word or to bear fruit from the words we receive. Like the church in Ephesus, we need to regularly repent of those things mentioned in Luke 8:

> "This is the meaning of the parable: The seed is the word of God. Those along the path are the ones who hear, and then the devil comes and takes away the word from their hearts, so that they may not believe and be saved. Those on the rocky ground are the ones who receive the word with joy when they hear it, but they have no root. They believe for a while, but in the *time of testing* they fall away. The seed that fell among thorns stands for those who hear, but as they go on their way they are choked by *life's worries, riches and*

> *pleasures*, and they do not mature" (Luke 8:11-14, emphasis added).

Do you need a "you-turn"? Do you need a change of thinking or attitude? Have the cares and worries of this life choked out your thoughts of God? Has a recent testing of your faith led to a "falling away" of your zeal and enthusiasm, similar to the conditions in Ephesus? Are you doing the deeds you've always done but in need of getting back to "the deeds you did at first"? If your answer is yes to any of those questions, then the word for you is *repent*. You need to turn and go in a different direction, but you won't be able to do that until you address your thoughts and attitudes.

This week, think about what it will take for you to make a "you-turn." Whatever it takes, I promise you will not change direction until you change your thinking. If and when you do, you will unlock the power in repentance—and that will earn you all the promises of God in Revelation for those who overcome.

Week #26

Your Word World

In this chapter, let's stay in the book of Revelation, which has much to say about our topic of unlocking the power of our thinking. In the last chapter, we looked at Jesus' promise to the Ephesian church if they would only have ears to hear. In this chapter, let's examine His promise to the church at Pergamum:

> "Whoever has ears, let them hear what the Spirit says to the churches. To the one who is victorious, I will give some of the hidden manna. I will also give that person a white stone with a new name written on it, known only to the one who receives it" (Revelation 2:17).

This promise always makes me think of what Jesus said to the disciples in John 4:32: "I have food to eat that you know nothing about." For Jesus, seeking and saving the lost was His "hidden manna," the purpose for which He had come. When He fulfilled it, it was more enjoyable and filling than actual food. The same is true for your purpose, but alas, I digress, for right now we want to look at what it means to have ears to hear.

THE WORD *WORLD*

I am teaching an online class on the four gospels for which students have to answer many essay questions. One of the questions goes something like this: "What are some examples of racism in the world?" I have had about 300 students come through the class and 295 of them have responded to the question by telling me about the situation in the United States. Only *five* have given me any *international* examples of racism. I'm not mocking or criticizing the students. My point is that when they see the word *world* they think about the *world* that is within their reach made up of their culture and friends. Because they have conditioned their mind to think like that, when I write *world*, they think U.S. Don't be too hard on the students, for you have the same tendency.

Take the word *generous*. The Bible clearly instructs us to be generous. But what does generous mean to you? If you had two suits, would generous be to give one away? Would generous really be to give both of them away and go without? If you think it's the first, then giving the second one would not even cross your mind—not even if the Lord prompted you to do it. The same can be true for words like *go, missions, forgive, pray*, and *give*. We approach those action words with preconceived thoughts of what they mean and how we should express them in our individual worlds.

BE CAREFUL

Jesus gave the disciples these instructions right after He explained the parable of the sower:

> "No one lights a lamp and hides it in a clay jar or puts it under a bed. Instead, they put it on a stand, so that those who come in can see the light. For there is nothing hidden that will not be disclosed, and nothing concealed that will not be known or brought out into the open. Therefore *consider carefully how you listen*. Whoever has will be given more; whoever does not have, even what they think they have will be taken from them" (Luke 8:16-18, emphasis added).

Jesus was indicating that His parables were not intended to hide or conceal but were teaching tools to reveal God's truth. Once the listeners understood those principles, it was their responsibility to reveal them to others as well and not conceal or bury them. If the disciples and people in the crowds weren't careful, they would hear, celebrate, and go home in the same or worse condition than when they arrived. The same is true for us today. We can hear a "good message or word," and applaud, cry, sing, and shout in response, but go home no different. Why? Because we were not careful how we listened. After Jesus said those words, His family suddenly came to visit. Jesus continued His lesson:

> Now Jesus' mother and brothers came to see him, but they were not able to get near him because of the crowd. Someone told him, "Your mother and brothers are standing outside, wanting to see you." He replied, "My mother and brothers are those who *hear God's word and put it into practice*" (Luke 8:19-21, emphasis added).

If you are serious about unlocking the power of your thinking, you must learn to challenge everything you know and hear. This is not so you can shoot holes in shallow concepts but to determine if there is anything preventing *you* from comprehending and then *doing* something with what you heard. That is what it means to have "ears that hear." If we return to the church at Pergamum, we see that Jesus promised one more thing for those who heard and acted on what they heard: "I will also give that person a white stone with a new name written on it, known only to the one who receives it."

If you learn to hear *and* do, God will give you a purpose no one else can see (that's the white stone mentioned in Revelation). It will be a phrase that others don't grasp or see but it moves you to tears. To get that purpose, however, you have to learn to pay attention to ensure you aren't depriving or shortchanging it of its full meaning like my students did to words like *world*. If you learn to do that, you will have truly unlocked the power of your thinking.

Week #27

The Mark

As we continue our journey in Revelation, let's look at a promise Jesus gave to the church at Philadelphia:

> "I am coming soon. Hold on to what you have, so that no one will take your crown. The one who is victorious I will make a pillar in the temple of my God. Never again will they leave it. I will write on them the name of my God and the name of the city of my God, the new Jerusalem, which is coming down out of heaven from my God; and I will also write on them my new name. Whoever has ears, let them hear what the Spirit says to the churches" (Revelation 3:11-13).

People through the ages have been fascinated and even infatuated with the concept that something is going to be written on their heads, and of course the 666 of Revelation 13:18 gets most of the attention. Let's examine this concept to see what we can learn as it pertains to our thought life.

THE MARK

It is no secret that we have made much of the 666 reference but when we read the next verse it says, "Then I [John] looked, and there before me was the Lamb, standing on Mount Zion, and with him 144,000 who had his name and his Father's name written on their foreheads" (Revelation 14:1). I have never heard a sermon or seen a book about the Father's name on our forehead but of course there is lots of material on 666. Yet what John saw in Revelation 14:1 coincides with the promise made to the Philadelphia church: God will write a new name on those who hold on, are victorious, and have ears to hear. They will be made pillars in the temple of their God.

What is the significance of the mark on the forehead? Jewish men often wear a small leather box strapped to their forehead (or arms) that contains a Hebrew text. They do this to remind them to obey the Law of God and always have it on their mind. In the New Testament, the Holy Spirit replaces the phylactery. Why would those who do not know the Lord have the number 666 instead of a phylactery? It is because the things of the world ruled by the evil one are always on their minds.

God empowers us through the Spirit to keep the things of God on our minds at all times. He has marked us as His. It was never intended to mean there would be a literal mark, but there would be something that separates the people of God from others. What is that mark? What distinguishes us from all others? It is faith, pure and simple. Those who have 666 will look for all sorts of means and formulas to provide for their needs. Those who have God's name "engraved' on their hearts and minds will look to Him. If they "forget," the Spirit will remind them.

FAITH IS THE KEY

Do you think God needs a physical mark to distinguish between those who are His and those who are not? Of course not! He recognizes them by their faith, to which God always responds: "And without faith it is impossible to please God, because anyone who comes to him must believe that he exists and that he rewards those who earnestly seek him" (Hebrews 11:6). If without faith it is impossible to please God, then with faith it is possible. Without faith, people will be scrambling for the crumbs that fall from the world's table. For those with faith, their God will set a sumptuous banquet table before them. Therefore, we could say that 666 is simply the symbol of unbelief while the name of God and His city given to those who hear and overcome are the marks of those who know Him through faith.

If you truly want to unlock the power of your thinking, don't look for a system or a formula. You should not pursue fads or copycat techniques (or bogus end-time fantasies) that will get you what you want or need—or feed your need for sci-fi adventure.

You are simply to strap on an invisible phylactery of faith and keep that before you at all times. Faith is what will unlock the power of your thinking because faith invites God into the process. Your faith relies on the Spirit to empower your thoughts but there is one caution: This is not a passive process. You must work to "take every thought captive to the obedience of Christ" (2 Corinthians 10:5).

Unlocking your thinking is not simply "I have given it all to the Lord" so you then wait for Him to fill your head. It involves work as you wrestle some of your thoughts to the ground, pin them, and then replace them with new thought champions. As you learn and grow, you will live in the principle we discussed many chapters ago: "be transformed by the renewing of your mind" (Romans 12:2). As you change your thoughts, you will transform your life and there will no need to worry about any mark except the mark of faith.

Week #28

Walking Down a Different Row

When I visit my grandchildren, there is a nearby farm where the public can go to pick fruit and vegetables. Not too long ago, I went there to pick some berries. It is hard work for this farm is on a hill. It was a hot summer day, and while the berry bushes had plenty of fruit, the many bushes were spread out over a large portion of the hillside. I found it fascinating that I could walk down one row with bushes on both sides of me and see plenty of fruit, but then when I went to the next row and looked back on the row I came from, I saw fruit I missed. I tried to see all there was to see when I went down the first row, but no matter how hard I tried, I could not see it all. What I needed was a change of perspective to see all there was to see—and pick.

When I have led cognitive and social learning seminars, I include a phrase, "When I change the way I look at things, the things I look at change." Of course, the things I'm looking at don't change, but my perspective is changed according to my approach and angle for viewing. I have used the same concept when I have taught preaching classes, for I tell students they must suspend what they *think* they know about a verse or passage for just a quick moment as they prepare to speak, for as soon as they are convinced that they know all that a passage has to say, they can miss what else it may be saying. This is called the lock-on, lock-out phenomenon. As soon as we lock on to what we think we know or see, certain we have seen all the berries or the meanings there are, we lock out the possibility of seeing more.

When I was a pastor and offered marriage counseling, I would surprise couples when we began by asking both parties to tell me what their partner was about to tell me about them. "What is your wife/husband going to tell me about you?" Many would make an effort to answer my question, but quickly switched gears to report what was wrong with their spouse. They had locked on to the problem with the other person and had often locked out their contribution to the flawed relationship and the need for counseling.

What's my point in all this? It's a valuable exercise to put yourself in someone else's place or to shift your perspective from time to time in order to see what you cannot see from where you have been. For example, recently I read a book titled *The Best Short Stories by Black Writers (1899-1967)*. Why would I order and read this? I did so because I am not black and I want to read something written by people who don't look like me and probably don't think like me. Since I work with many African Americans, it may help me walk down a different row to see what I could not previously see.

When we don't walk down a different row, it may be because we are not as secure in who we are or what we believe as we would like others to believe and thus need to read or be exposed only to things that will reinforce our current position. That's not wrong unless it is what we always do and thereby cut ourselves off from the "fruit" that is right in front of us, but we can't see. This blindness isn't because we aren't physically capable or don't want to see, but simply because we cannot see it from where we are standing—mentally or physically.

Do you have the courage to walk down a different row and see something new? Or will you keep walking up and down the same old row and limit yourself to what you are convinced is all there is to see? While you are answering those questions, I will be reading a book just like the one I described earlier to get a different perspective on what I thought I already knew.

Week #29

Leper Lessons

One of my favorite Bible stories is found in 2 Kings 7. The Arameans, the enemies of Israel, had laid siege to the city and the people inside were starving to death. That's when four lepers, who knew they were going to die if they just stayed where they were, decided to go out and meet the enemy to see if they could obtain mercy—and some food. We read,

> Now there were four leprous men at the entrance of the gate; and they said to one another, "Why do we sit here until we die? "If we say, 'We will enter the city,' then the famine is in the city and we will die there; and if we sit here, we die also. Now therefore come, and let us go over to the camp of the Arameans. If they spare us, we will live; and if they kill us, we will but die." At dusk they got up and went to the camp of the Arameans. When they reached the edge of the camp, no one was there, for the Lord had caused the Arameans to hear the sound of chariots and horses and a great army, so that they said to one another, "Look, the king of Israel has hired the Hittite and Egyptian kings to attack us!" So they got up and fled in the dusk and abandoned their tents and their horses and donkeys. They left the camp as it was and ran for their lives (2 Kings 7:3-4).

The lepers returned to the city to tell the people the good news, but the city inhabitants thought their story was a trap to lure them out from behind the walls so therefore they did not respond right away, even though they were dying.

WHAT'S TIMING TO A LEPER?

The four lepers saw their condition as critical. They were less concerned about looking bad or "missing God" than survival. It is *not* faith to want to know the timing and steps you will need to take to succeed. It is actually presumptuous. God does *not* owe you a full explanation before you take the first steps in obedience. To think that He does is to expect more than He gave Abraham when God told Abraham to leave his homeland. When Abraham wanted to know where he was going, the Lord basically responded, "I'll tell you when you get there."

If you don't identify with the lepers, you will say that you can "wait on the Lord." However, if you do identify with their situation and see yourself like them in desperate need to have faith and act, then you will step out today and act on your creativity, ideas, goals, and dreams. Have you had enough of being where you are? Then do something and be less concerned about timing and more concerned about finding fulfillment and creative expression—and being productive for the Lord.

Let me close with one more thought. I hear people regularly say, "I don't want to get ahead of the Lord." My response is always the same: Go ahead and try. If Ephesians 3:20-21 is true (and it is), there is *no way* you can get ahead of Him:

> Now to him who is able to do immeasurably more than all we ask or imagine, according to his power that is at work within us, to him be glory in the church and in Christ Jesus throughout all generations, for ever and ever! Amen.

If you can think it, then God is already thinking bigger. Dream big and then step out to see what happens. Give yourself permission to move out, knowing you can't get ahead of God and you won't fully please Him *until* you act in faith, faith that your time is *now* to do the will of God. In your newfound freedom, I trust you will find the freedom to unlock the power of your thinking that only a leper's perspective can bring.

Week #30

Stop To-Do List

I had a weekly one-hour radio show on a local AM Christian station called *Wake Up to Purpose* for four years. It was a joy to produce and do, even though I had to get up at 5:30 a.m., get to the station, and then after the show drive across town to teach a class. What's more, I paid for the privilege of having many wonderful guests on the show who told their purpose stories, and always received great feedback from listeners. Yet after four years of on-the-air success, I decided to end the show. At the same time, I also decided to *stop* writing a daily devotional which I had produced for six years.

Why would I stop doing things I loved that seemed to be helping others, even though all the feedback was positive and others wanted me to continue? I did so because I have learned it's important not only to have a *to-do* list, but also a *stop-to-do* list. If you are serious about unlocking the power of your thinking, then you need to pay closer attention to things you should *stop* doing as well as what you *should* do.

THE STATUS QUO

As mentioned earlier, you and I have all the time in the world—24 hours every day we are alive. We cannot get any more time, so we have to make decisions, sometimes difficult decisions, to stop doing something to create space for something new. The challenge is that often we don't know what the new things will be, so we hold on to the old out of fear—fear that we won't find the new, that the new won't be as good as the old, or that the new will not work out. Therefore, we clutch and claw to hold on to the status quo, when truth be told, the status quo has often become stale and outdated. Here are some other thoughts about the status quo:

1. **You may think maintaining your status quo is not**

a decision, but it is. When you are considering several change options and don't choose any of them, it seems like you have not made a decision. You have, however, decided not to change.

2. **Choosing the status quo costs you something**. You may have chosen the safety of what you know, but you lost all the possibilities of what the new can bring.
3. **The status quo may not be all that good; it's just safe**. Ask yourself this question about the status quo: If you didn't have this status quo, would you go out of your way again to create it? Would you apply again for your current job? Would you buy your current dwelling again? Would you have pursued this career if you had known back then what you know today? If the answers are no, then perhaps it's time to start thinking not about how to preserve the present but to create a more desirable future.

CREATE SPACE

It's time for you to create some space for the new, even if you aren't sure what all that new is—like I did with the radio and devotional. It's time to make time to write because you want to write, but currently don't have the time—or won't allow yourself to find the time (because you are afraid). It's time to give yourself time to breathe and think, and that means stopping the old so you can discover the new—or so the new can discover you.

Whenever you are reading this, treat the day like it is December 31 and you are on the verge of a new year. Did you do what you said you were going to do one year ago? Has this been an exhilarating year of new tastes and smells, or has it seemed like you are eating stale bread? I invite you to join me in creating space for the new by jettisoning some of the old cargo to which you are clinging for dear life. I don't know what the year ahead will bring, but I hope it's not what the last years brought if it was just more of the same that made you unhappy or unfulfilled.

If you think about stopping the old to make room for the new, it doesn't mean you have to stop or start anything. It simply means you are willing to do so and then God is able to direct you to new thoughts that could lead to new behaviors. If your status quo is locked in chains, then perhaps it's time to unlock it by unleashing the power of new thoughts we have discussed throughout this book.

Week #31

What Are You Wearing Right Now?

On an older version of my website, I had a purpose assessment questionnaire that asked people how often they searched for clues to help them know what their purpose is or is is not. My goal was to have them pay attention to their heart and not to their thoughts of what others expected or wanted them to do or be.

It's difficult to walk in someone else's expectations, especially when those expectations don't relate to your purpose or the gifts and talents you have. You can try to please society, your family, and even your own expectations of what you *think* you should be or do, but eventually you will fail. It will deplete your energy and creativity and you will be miserable—and only you will know. So what's the answer? How can you unlock the power of your thinking where you and your purpose are concerned?

It's simple—just don't do it.

You must resist when someone, well-meaning or otherwise, tries to get you to fulfill their vision for your life. You must learn to have and pursue your own vision, for it is the only road to happiness and success, and one of the road signs for that vision or purpose is the joy or lack of it in your own heart. That's what David had to do before he was king and it served him well. You may want to read the story to which I am referring in 1 Samuel 17 before we proceed.

TRY THIS ON

The story of David and Goliath is known in many cultures and lands. Every day, Goliath and the armies of Israel would line up across from one another and nothing would happen. One day, David came to check up on his brothers and heard Goliath taunting the armies of Israel. That angered him and caused him to wonder why no one was doing anything about it.

When he heard that there was a reward for anyone who would kill Goliath, David immediately volunteered to do the deed. When David told King Saul that he [David] would be the one to kill Goliath, Saul laughed, dismissing him as too young and inexperienced. David would not relent, so Saul eventually gave in and sanctioned the encounter. Before he let David go, however, he gave David his personal armor to wear:

> Then Saul dressed David in his own tunic. He put a coat of armor on him and a bronze helmet on his head. David fastened on his sword over the tunic and tried walking around, because he was not used to them. "I cannot go in these," he said to Saul, "because I am not used to them." So he took them off. Then he took his staff in his hand, chose five smooth stones from the stream, put them in the pouch of his shepherd's bag and, with his sling in his hand, approached the Philistine (1 Samuel 17:38-40).

David could not function in Saul's armor because Saul was a head taller than all his peers (see 1 Samuel 9:2). Instead, David took off the armor and took up what he felt most comfortable with—a slingshot and some stones.

WHAT ARE YOU WEARING RIGHT NOW?

Do you see the lesson here? Saul assumed that David could only fight dressed in body armor, so Saul gave him his. Perhaps others have tried to give you what fits them, and you have tried to walk in it. It's not possible, however, for you to be a man or woman of purpose and walk in what someone else gives you. You must find your own joy, creativity, and passion.

What's more, you can't explain it to anyone so they can understand when you don't even understand it. You just know what your heart is telling you and that is what you pursue, whether it makes perfect sense or not. Remember what the wisdom writer told us: "Each heart knows its own bitterness, and *no one else* can share its joy (Proverbs 14:10 emphasis added).

You know how much you love music, art, travel, writing,

business, preaching, or medicine. No one knows better than you what's in your heart, no matter how much they love you or well-intentioned they are. Only you are equipped to hear and follow your heart. Are you up to the task? Are you ready to reject the thoughts of others where you are concerned and accept your own? That is the only way you can unlock your potential as you unlock the power of your thinking where you are concerned.

This week, it's time to be honest. Are you trying to fulfill someone else's expectations for you? Have you put on someone else's armor? If so, take it off immediately and that means to replace the thought armor belonging to someone else and replace it with your slingshot-and-stone one. Don't face your Goliaths this week in someone else's image for you. Face them in your own; that is good enough to get the job done. You will feel lighter, nimbler, and happier than you have been in a while, and it will be a significant step to identify and embrace your purpose.

Week #32

Talk the Walk

Have you ever said something about yourself or referred to something you wanted to do and then thought, "Why did I say that? What are people thinking of me right now? They must think I'm boasting or have a big ego!" If so, then that may be why you can't clarify your purpose, simply because you are not comfortable talking about or referring to yourself. Don't worry, however, for there is someone who can help you with this kind of thinking.

DID HE REALLY SAY THAT?

In the last chapter, we saw that David could not wear Saul's armor when he went out to face Goliath. He had to wear and use what was most comfortable for him. In the same way, you cannot walk in someone else's expectations or purpose for you, no matter how well-intentioned they may be. So David, armed with the right equipment (a sling and some stones), stepped onto the battlefield to face this fearsome giant. Immediately he was confronted with the behemoth uttering some daunting threats:

> He said to David, "Am I a dog, that you come at me with sticks?" And the Philistine cursed David by his gods. "Come here," he said, "and I'll give your flesh to the birds of the air and the beasts of the field!" (1 Samuel 17:43-44).

Now if David was like some people I know, he would have then said, "Well, maybe, I mean perhaps the Lord may want to use me, but don't get me wrong, I'm not saying I know for sure and if something good does happen, it will be the Lord and not me. I don't want you to *ever* think it's me." Fortunately, David was of a different mindset. When Goliath verbally attacked him, David was quick to retaliate:

> "You come against me with sword and spear and javelin, but I come against you in the name of the Lord Almighty, the God of the armies of Israel, whom you have defied. This day the Lord will hand you over to me, and I'll strike you down and cut off your head. Today I will give the carcasses of the Philistine army to the birds of the air and the beasts of the earth, and the whole world will know that there is a God in Israel. All those gathered here will know that it is not by sword or spear that the Lord saves; for the battle is the Lord's, and he will give all of you into our hands" (1 Samuel 17:45-47).

What bravado! What courage! What confidence David had! There was nothing tentative in what he said or planned to do. He was bold and specific. Some think that kind of talk alienates God and you may be one of them. If so, then you need to change the way you think. God isn't repelled by such talk. That talk drew God to David's cause and He promptly went out with David to meet the giant. David made good on his promises, while Goliath died trying to figure out what went wrong.

TALK THE WALK

How can you apply this lesson to your life right now to unlock the power of your thinking? First, David had a track record from which he could draw. He had killed lions and bears, and he saw killing this giant as a continuation and outgrowth of those exploits. You must allow God to put you in challenging situations so that when you overcome, you will be able to refer back to those experiences to help you fight future battles. Or, if you have past exploits, you need to remember those lessons and bring them into your current life challenges.

Second, you must know who you are and what you want to do. David did not hold back; he was clear and concise. He said, "I am a champion of God and you, Goliath, are not. You are coming down, in spite of your size, words, and confidence." Finally, David said what he was going to do without fear of what others thought of him. He spoke positive, affirming, and powerful words and then set about fulfilling them, even though he was young—a lot younger than all those soldiers, his brothers, and King Saul.

What are you speaking these days? A better question is what *aren't* you speaking? Tentative, faithless words produce tentative, faithless actions. Positive, powerful words produce similar actions. Stop being hesitant and afraid to make bold statements where your purpose and dreams are concerned. Dream great things, talk about them, and don't worry about how you sound to other people. You should only be concerned with how you sound to God.

Many people are concerned with walking the talk, but if you aren't talking about what you are going to do with God's help, you won't have anything to walk. Dream great things, talk about doing them, and then go for it. I know it's simple to describe but not simple to do. I also know you can only do great things once you stop stumbling and mumbling your way through your purpose and dreams. Every day this week, watch what you don't say and follow David's example to speak words of faith and courage as you transform your thinking about doing and talking about doing great things for God.

Week #33

What to Do with a Big Head

When someone describes someone else as having a big head, what do they mean? It usually means they have an inflated opinion of themselves. In other words, their thinking where they are concerned is conceited and, if they talk about themselves, it is even more of an indication that they have a "big head."

What do you do to avoid a "big head?" You may deny it when someone compliments you concerning something you do or are. You don't want to appear proud or egocentric, so you may minimize your strengths and achievements in your eyes and in the eyes of others—or deny them altogether. This may seem spiritual or noble, but it's actually indicates you need to unlock the power of your thinking where your image of yourself is concerned.

What *should* you do when you succeed or receive a compliment? I'm glad you asked. For the answer, however, you will have to read on.

A BIG HEAD

We have looked at the story of David and Goliath in the last two chapters. We saw how David made specific declarations of what he was about to do to Goliath. David made good on his promises and killed Goliath with one stone from his slingshot. It's what he did next that answers the questions I raised above. What did David do after he killed Goliath? He cut off his head! That must have been one oversized head not only to cut off but also to carry around.

The armies of Israel were encouraged by David's triumph, and went forth to secure their own victory over the Philistine army. That was one of the byproducts of David's success. Then David did something else that would be quite uncharacteristic for many I know, perhaps even for you:

> David took the Philistine's head and brought it to Jerusalem, and he put the Philistine's weapons in his own tent (1 Samuel 17:54).

What did David do with the head? I doubt if he kept it in his tent or made a keychain out of it. He did what most champions did with such spoils of battle. David probably hung the head on a post for everyone to see. David celebrated his own victory and advertised his achievement. What's more, he kept a souvenir of the battle by keeping the giant's sword in his trophy case. How does this answer the question of what to do when you achieve success? What insight does this give you into how you should respond when you receive a compliment?

DON'T WORRY THAT A BIG HEAD WILL GIVE YOU A BIG HEAD

David celebrated his victory. He wanted people to see Goliath's head so they would be encouraged to fight their own future battles. As a good leader, David wanted the people to see they didn't have to cower in fear. What's more, he didn't minimize his success by saying something like, "Well, it was nothing. It was a lucky shot and God really did it, not me."

Instead, David said, "Look what I've done. What can you do? What can we do together as an army without fear" That's what you need to do as well. If someone compliments you on something you've done or for something you are, say, "Thank you." Don't push their praise away.

If you have done something and no one compliments you, then compliment yourself. Admire what you've done and savor the moment, without being self-conscious or worrying about what others will think of you—if they need to know at all. If you achieve a goal for which you have worked hard, throw yourself a party and invite your friends to celebrate with you. Take a trip in honor of your new job, degree, or completed project.

David knew how to celebrate his victories and use them to spur himself and others on to greater things. We need to do the same. Don't worry about a big head; there will be enough tough knocks and challenges to keep your feet firmly planted in reality and your head to its normal hat size. When you do something great, however, don't be afraid to acknowledge it was significant. And if others acknowledge it as well and are inspired to their own greatness, then it is all the better.

This whole process may help you see that you may not be afraid of failure, but of what you will do if and when you succeed. That is an important way to unlock the power of your thinking. Can you handle success and the admiration of others? I hope you will learn to broadcast your victories rather than hide behind mediocrity so no one is offended. Aim for great things, do them, and tell the world if others don't.

Week #34

Christian-itis

Since 2006, I have written my thoughts and ideas in a journal notebook. In this chapter, I want to give you a reason why journaling is so important. The reason is that it fights off the disease called Christian-itis. You have never heard of Christian-itis? It's a serious condition that afflicts the mind and is capable of shutting down all your goal setting and purpose-seeking efforts, eventually causing a paralysis of your will. Let's look at this debilitating but not deadly disease.

TWO SYMPTOMS

Christian-itis usually manifests in one of two ways. The first is an inability to think or talk about yourself, what you enjoy, or what you are good at doing. To do so is pride, or so Christian-itis tells you, so you avoid doing any deep searching or digging. Christian-itis also warns you your feelings can lead you down the wrong path, so they aren't to be trusted. Compliments cannot be received and processed, for any achievements you have had are solely due to God's work in your life. Failures, on the other hand, are purely your fault and you must beat yourself up for any wrongs done and avoid doing anything similar to the events that led to the failure.

Another way Christian-itis manifests is in extreme passivity. This symptom dictates that you must wait on the Lord for all things, careful to avoid any initiatives that come from your heart or emotions. If God wants you to do or be something, then it is up to Him to initiate, confirm, direct, guide, and finalize everything. You are the passenger along for the ride and He is the captain, steward, purser, navigator, and entertainer. This symptom helps you avoid any failure but also any success, and it empowers you to judge the efforts of others rather than engage in your own. I am being facetious by exaggerating these symptoms, but not by much. Let's now look at how journaling can help you overcome Christian-itis and unlock the power of your thinking that will combat and overcome it.

PAY ATTENTION

Journaling helps you pay attention to what is going on around and in your mind and heart. Why is that important? It is critical to pay attention because that is how God communicates to you. You want to write down what you think and feel so you can see them, honor them, and allow God to use them to direct you in your paths of righteousness. Faith without actions is dead according to James and journaling gives you a chance to do *something* with your dreams, thoughts, and faith ideas. Read what the Lord told the prophet who was complaining to Him about his circumstances:

> I will stand at my watch and station myself on the ramparts; I will look to see what he will say to me, and what answer I am to give to this complaint. Then the Lord replied: "Write down the revelation and make it plain on tablets so that a herald may run with it. For the revelation awaits an appointed time; it speaks of the end and will not prove false. Though it linger, wait for it; it will certainly come and will not delay. See, he is puffed up; his desires are not upright—but the righteous will live by his faith" (Habakkuk 2:1-4).

If the Lord directed the prophet to write it down, don't you think He may be giving you the same advice?

I am including in the Appendix some journaling tips I found online to help you understand the journaling concept more fully. Yet there is no way to journal but to do it—and please don't use a yellow tablet or spiral notebook as a journal. Invest in something nice you will be sure to use. Get started this week and we will look in the next chapter at more advice to help you unlock the power of your thinking through journaling.

Week #35

Pay Attention

If you are going to unlock the power of your thinking, you must pay close attention to your thinking. It is almost like having an out-of-the-body experience that enables you to observe yourself. That may sound unusual, but in essence it means you must think about what you think about and discover the reasons why you are thinking it. To better understand what I mean and how to engage this process, it will be necessary for you to read on.

"WHO TOUCHED ME?"

There are many stories from Jesus' life and ministry that intrigue me. Here is one of them:

> A large crowd followed and pressed around him. And a woman was there who had been subject to bleeding for twelve years. She had suffered a great deal under the care of many doctors and had spent all she had, yet instead of getting better she grew worse. When she heard about Jesus, she came up behind him in the crowd and touched his cloak, because she thought, "If I just touch his clothes, I will be healed." Immediately her bleeding stopped and she felt in her body that she was freed from her suffering. At once Jesus realized that power had gone out from him. He turned around in the crowd and asked, "Who touched my clothes?" "You see the people crowding against you," his disciples answered, "and yet you can ask, 'Who touched me?' "But Jesus kept looking around to see who had done it (Mark 5:24b-32).

Jesus was so in touch with his surroundings that He knew when someone with a need touched Him. I am sometimes not aware that someone is in need when they tell me, but Jesus knew just by a touch. He could feel that something had happened, although for some reason the Son of Man did not know who it was (or perhaps He knew but wanted the woman to speak up for herself since she had tried to maintain her anonymity). I relate this verse to one found in Proverbs where seeking your purpose is concerned: "Each heart knows its own bitterness, and no one else can share its joy" (Proverbs 14:10). So how is this verse related to the passage from Mark 5?

PAY ATTENTION TO YOUR HEART

If you are searching for purpose or for the answer to any life situation, you must pay attention to what touches you or takes something from you. If you help an elderly person and you have unspeakable joy, you must ask, "Who and what just touched me? Why am I so exhilarated?" If you create art and it's a spiritual and emotional high for you, you must ask, "Why do I love it so?" If you are in a job that everyone says you should love but you don't, you have to ask, "Why am I so unhappy? What's missing here? What do I know that others don't about my heart?"

If you are going to find and fulfill your purpose, you must stop talking yourself out of or into how you think you should feel. You must pay closer attention than ever before to your own bitterness and joy and start asking questions like, "What just touched me and why did I feel so good (or bad)?"

I stopped trying to make myself enjoy something I don't. I stopped listening to others tell me why I should be joyful when I was not. I stopped trying to explain why I loved doing something or going somewhere when others didn't feel the same thing or even understand what I was sensing. In other words, I started paying attention to and stopped apologizing for who I am. I stopped using my thoughts to talk myself out of who I am and into who I am not and will never be.

Are you ready to follow my example? Are you ready to pay attention to your thoughts and current reality and then do something about what you love and don't love? Are you ready to stop apologizing for who you are? Are you ready to stop following others' expectations and follow your heart? If you are, then you will surely find your purpose and be productive for the Lord. God wants you to know and, if you will stop fighting it in your mind, you cannot help but find it, probably with the evidence from the encounters with your own heart and experience as you have those out-of-the-body experiences I mentioned at the start of this chapter.

Week #36

Keep Pouring

Have you ever faced economic pressure that almost paralyzed you? You were in such desperate straits that you did not know what to do next? In 2001, I faced a major life transition when I started PurposeQuest International. The pressure was so great that there were days I did nothing but lay on the couch. We had no money, I had no business, and I wasn't always sure what to do next. If you are facing something like this or have faced it, then perhaps you can relate. If you haven't, you may want to read on and then file this away for future use, just in case you need it—and chances are in your own quest for purpose you will face this kind of pressure at one time or another.

MORE JARS

In 2 Kings 4, the prophet Elisha met a widow who was also in desperate times. She was so heavily in debt that she feared losing her son to her creditors. When she sought out God's prophet for advice, Elisha gave her some unexpected counsel. He told her to go and find as many jars as possible. Once she had done that, she was to go home, close the door, and start pouring the little oil she had into those jars. Here is what happened next:

> She left him and afterward shut the door behind her and her sons. They brought the jars to her and she kept pouring. When all the jars were full, she said to her son, "Bring me another one." But he replied, "There is not a jar left." Then the oil stopped flowing. She went and told the man of God, and he said, "Go, sell the oil and pay your debts. You and your sons can live on what is left" (2 Kings 4:5-7).

Do you think the woman wished at that point she had gathered more jars to hold the oil? The point is that you must still operate in faith when you are desperate. What's more, you must do things consistent not with where you are now but where you will be when your breakthrough comes, and that breakthrough will come as you unlock the power of your thinking not to focus on the crisis but on God's promise and His solution.

MY JARS

When I had that desperate time, I could barely function, but I knew I had to get up off the couch and write. I had to prepare seminars and teachings even though I had no business. I had to make financial decisions for the future when I had no money in the present. What's more, I felt directed to give away things to others when my own needs were critical. It was during that season when I began writing my weekly update called the *Monday Memo* and gave it away to anyone who was interested. Shortly thereafter, I began to send out my weekly Bible studies free of charge to any and all. I designed a website and committed money to its development, money I didn't have with no promise of any return once it was up and running.

Now that I look back, I did what this woman did many centuries ago: I kept pouring what little I had and God kept providing more. I am teaching today what I developed in those dark, uncertain times. I meet with hundreds of people every year from all over the world, and I counsel them with things I read about and studied when my financial pressure almost rendered me helpless and without hope.

So what about you? Are you in a time that seems to call for despair? If so, maybe it's time to gather some more jars and start pouring? Your situation may be critical, but I urge you to think and act this week like it isn't. I am asking you to do what only God can help you do: act today like your breakthrough is already here, even though the evidence says otherwise. If you can do this, then when your breakthrough comes, and it will come, you will have enough jars—whatever that represents for you—to hold the blessings that are in store for every purposeful servant of God. If I made it through my dark time, you will, too. When it's all over, you will be glad you didn't stop pouring, glad you didn't succumb to thoughts of despair and instead held on to thoughts of hope and purpose.

Week #37

A Few Sticks

Have you ever faced what you considered a hopeless situation? Are you facing one now? In the last few chapters, we have looked at the role of economic hardship as a means either to scare you off your purpose or to refine you along the way. In this chapter, I want to continue that theme and look at a woman who had given up hope, who was ready to go home and die. She was thinking thoughts of doom and gloom and God had to give her some new thoughts to unlock her thinking's power if she was going to make it through. If you are about to give up, read on. If you aren't facing that scenario yet, read on anyway, for you may face that kind of hopelessness one day.

A FEW STICKS

The Lord sent the prophet Elijah to a woman in 1 Kings 17 during a famine. The woman did not know it at the time but she was going to feed Elijah during the drought and, while feeding Elijah, she would feed her family as well. Sometimes God wants you to be generous when every thought in you says that isn't possible.

Elijah came face to face with the woman and asked her for a drink. We know she was generous, for she gave the man some water even though there was a severe drought. Then Elijah asked her for some bread. When he did, this is what she said:

> "As surely as the Lord your God lives," she replied, "I don't have any bread—only a handful of flour in a jar and a little oil in a jug. I am gathering a few sticks to take home and make a meal for myself and my son, that we may eat it—and die" (1 Kings 17:12).

This woman was thinking, "It's over. Things could not

possibly get any worse. Death is the next step." Yet Elijah told her that she had seen the worst and things were going to get better. He gave her new thoughts and perspective:

> Elijah said to her, "Don't be afraid. Go home and do as you have said. But first make a small cake of bread for me from what you have and bring it to me, and then make something for yourself and your son. For this is what the Lord, the God of Israel, says: 'The jar of flour will not be used up and the jug of oil will not run dry until the day the Lord gives rain on the land'" (1 Kings 17:13-14).

And that is exactly what happened. That woman went from having a few sticks and a piece of bread to an endless supply of food for her, her son, and the prophet.

SCARCITY MENTALITY

When things have been tough, you naturally switch into survival mode. This woman was just trying to survive and she had run out of hope for that. The thought of prosperity was out of the question. Yet her breakthrough was just a moment away. What's more, your breakthrough may be only a chance meeting, a phone call, or an idea away as well.

Notice that Elijah told the woman what Moses told the Israelites when they were in the desert: Don't be afraid. Fear will cripple you in a crisis and you need all your creativity and hope to make it through the tough times. Those times come to prove that God is faithful and to make you resilient and hopeful. But you must be hopeful not in your own efforts or ideas, but in God.

If you aren't facing this kind of hopelessness, then perhaps you know someone who is. If you are, I'm not advising you to ignore the severity of your situation. I am urging you, however, not to lose hope even when your reason for hope is totally obscured. Say what Job said, "Though he slay me, yet will I hope in him" (Job 13:15), and keep on keeping on. Then one day I hope you will write your story and send it to me so that others may be encouraged who feel that all they have is a few sticks standing between them and utter failure.

Week #38

Fleeced

If you are like some believers, you want to know if your ideas and actions are sanctioned by the Lord. Thus, you may seek for a sign of confirmation before you act, and that whole process is called putting out a fleece before the Lord. We first saw that idea in the story of Gideon, so let's look at that now and see if there are any lessons we can learn from what Gideon did and why he did it to help us unlock the power of our thinking.

FLEECED

God appeared to Gideon and designated him as the one to deliver Israel from the Midianites. This directive was not what Gideon was expecting, so he asked God on three separate occasions to give him a sign that it was indeed the Lord who was guiding his steps. Here is one of those instances:

> Gideon said to God, "If you will save Israel by my hand as you have promised—Look, I will place a wool fleece on the threshing floor. If there is dew only on the fleece and all the ground is dry, then I will know that you will save Israel by my hand, as you said." And that is what happened. Gideon rose early the next day; he squeezed the fleece and wrung out the dew—a bowlful of water. Then Gideon said to God, "Do not be angry with me. Let me make just one more request. Allow me one more test with the fleece. This time make the fleece dry and the ground covered with dew." That night God did so. Only the fleece was dry; all the ground was covered with dew (Judges 6:36-40).

You see from this passage that a fleece before the Lord was

just that for Gideon: a sheep's skin that one time was drenched with dew and another time wasn't. Gideon selected that specific sign and God chose to respond. It would be nice if God would respond to every request for confirmation like He did in this instance, but He usually doesn't. Why is that?

It's because most requests are made not in faith but in unbelief and God does not respond very well to those who don't trust Him in the first place. When that happens, they get the response Jesus gave to the Jews. Let's look at that now.

NO SIGN, SORT OF

> Then some of the Pharisees and teachers of the law said to him, "Teacher, we want to see a miraculous sign from you." He answered, "A wicked and adulterous generation asks for a miraculous sign! But none will be given it except the sign of the prophet Jonah" (Matthew 12:38-39).

Notice that Jesus didn't really say there would be no sign. Instead, He said it would be a sign of God's choosing and the sign would be that Jesus be raised from the dead after three days, just as Jonah was delivered after three days of being in the belly of the big fish. The problem with asking for a sign today is that a sign has already been given: Jesus is alive!

You see, if God can raise the dead, then He can do anything. He can help you start your business, publish your work, find you a job, or fund your missions trip. When you say, "Oh God, I need a sign to let me know whether or not this is something You want me to do," you run the danger of asking because you don't really believe you can do what you are being asked to do. You are asking in doubt and unbelief and not faith. Faith is always a decision and not a feeling, although your feelings will confirm the rightness of your decision to walk in faith. Your thinking plays a major role in your faith walk.

The Lord asked Gideon to lead a battle against a significant foe and Gideon needed that reassurance because many lives were on the line. Most of us won't ever face that kind of challenge.

Yours is much less demanding, so the knowledge that God raises the dead assures you God can do anything, especially helping you do what's in your heart—like writing poetry, making a commitment to feed the hungry, or starting a business.

Perhaps this week you need to stop procrastinating in unbelief by putting out a fleece which will never be answered because you have all the sign you need or are going to receive. Rather than waste your time waiting, be looking for ways to do what is in your heart to do. When you do that, God will send you all the confirmation you need at every step of the way.

Week #39

Pipe Dreams

When it comes to purpose, vision, and goals, people have dreams and some share them with me. I had someone tell me he wanted to own a television station, another tell me he wanted to give $100 million away one day, and still another that she wanted to have a chain of homes for abused children and women. While I listen politely and do all I can to encourage them, I'm thinking all the while, "This is nothing but a pipe dream." A pipe dream is an unrealistic hope or expectation, but until today, I didn't know the origin of the phrase until I did some research. Do you want to know where the phrase "pipe dream" came from? If you do or don't, you know the rules—you will have to read on.

WHAT ARE YOU SMOKING?

The phrase "pipe dream" came from the dreams some people had when they smoked opium in the 19th century. After they imbibed, they would have strange visions and some creative works like the poem *Kubla Khan* were said to be the result of the author being under the influence of opium. There is another question among the young today when they hear someone make an outlandish statement when they ask, "What are you smoking?" which is an obvious reference to someone who isn't in full control of their faculties.

Now that you know the source, you may not think it fair on my part to refer to some people's dreams as pipe dreams, but I maintain it is accurate. This is not because they are on drugs but because their dream is totally and completely unrealistic. You see, God cannot give you what you are not ready to receive. If you have not developed your potential, God cannot and will not promote you, no matter how much faith you have. Let's consider the examples I mentioned in the opening paragraph.

The man who wanted to own a television station had no experience in business or media for that matter. He worked in an unrelated job and had no concept of what television was all about, nor was he prepared to learn. The man who wanted to give $100 million away was playing the lottery, instead of being involved in jobs or training that could teach him how to manage and distribute large sums of money. The woman who wanted to earn a chain of homes was not even working with the abused or afflicted when she shared her dream with me. In each case, the dreamer was not doing what they could do while expecting God to do His part. They had put all the burden of seeing their dream fulfilled on Him while exempting themselves from taking the necessary steps. In other words, their thinking was wrong.

None of the people in those three examples was doing anything to prepare themselves for their dream. They were like people who were believing for a best-selling book but never write or develop their writing skills. They all had pipe dreams in the Lord and they were just as fantastic as someone who was on a hallucinatory drug. In a way, their dreams were making them think they were doing something when in reality they were not.

SUCCESS IS NO ACCIDENT

While success requires heaps of faith, it also requires preparation. David learned to lead and protect sheep and that prepared him to be king. Saul was a Hebrew scholar and that enabled him, with God's help, to be Saint Paul. Some experts estimate it requires 10,000 hours invested in any one discipline or skill to be ready for success. In my own life, I have interviewed and counseled thousands of people over the last thirty years to help them find their purpose. I have written, read, talked, and taught about purpose and creativity. I have debated, been contradicted and dismissed as wrong, made friends, lost friends, traveled the world, and gone to school. Those were the things I could do while I have trusted God to do the things only He could do. Even then, whatever I achieved has been a result of His grace, but His grace would not open the door if I was not prepared to walk through it.

What is your dream and purpose? If you know, then you must do all you can do to see it happen in God's will and timing. If you are believing for an airplane, you can at least learn to fly. If you will travel, you can at least get a passport and learn some words in the language of the culture to which you are headed. Pipe dreams are just fantasies but faith dreams are real because faith is real, the substance of things hoped for. And we also know James wrote, "You see that a person is justified by what he does and not by faith alone" (James 2:24).

The Chinese say a journey of a thousand miles begins with the first step. Are you ready to take the first step or, if you have already, the next step in your faith journey? Are you prepared to take another step every day, no matter how many steps you have remaining between you and your dream? I hope so. If you are, then you are a candidate for greatness and you have unlocked the power of your thinking that will enable you to achieve. If not, then all you may have is a pipe dream, and pipe dreams may make for good poetry, but they seldom achieve the end result.

Week #40

Hiding from God

In this chapter, let's consider the story of King Saul's ascent to leadership in 1 Samuel. There are many puzzling things about Saul's leadership journey as recorded that cause me to ask questions like,

- Why did God seem so supportive of Saul's appointment, even though He was clear that Saul represented Israel's rejection of His kingship?
- Why did Saul seem so spiritual at one point with so many supernatural confirmations of his leadership and then fall and fail so quickly?
- Why was Samuel so ready to reject Saul as king when Saul disobeyed over what was seemingly much less of a transgression than David committed with Bathsheba?

I'm not sure I will find definitive answers, but I know I will enjoy the investigation and attempt to connect the answers to our current theme of unlocking the power of our thinking.

LESSONS TO LEARN

One thing stood out to me right away as I began to study and that was how ambivalent Saul was about the leadership position God was assigning him. While it seemed humble and the proper response, I'm not sure it was, and I believe it is a common response among God's people:

1. **Excuses:** "Saul answered, 'But am I not a Benjamite, from the smallest tribe of Israel, and is not my clan the least of all the clans of the tribe of Benjamin? Why do you say such a thing to me?'" (1 Samuel

9:21). Like Gideon, Saul objected that his family heritage was not worthy of leadership and tried to use low self-esteem as an excuse not to lead.

2. **Silence**: "Saul's uncle said, 'Tell me what Samuel said to you.' Saul replied, 'He assured us that the donkeys had been found.' But he did not tell his uncle what Samuel had said about the kingship" (1 Samuel 10:14-16). Saul refused to tell his uncle what God had said to him through Samuel, perhaps assuming his silence would cause the entire encounter with Samuel to go away.
3. **Hiding**: "Finally Saul son of Kish was taken. But when they looked for him, he was not to be found. So they inquired further of the Lord, 'Has the man come here yet?' And the Lord said, 'Yes, he has hidden himself among the supplies'" (1 Samuel 10:21b-22). After he had no other way to avoid God's call and assignment, Saul resorted to hiding in the warehouse. He thought he could hide from God's plan, and it would all just go away, but he was wrong. God's choice was clear and final, and Saul would reluctantly accept the call. I wonder if the rest of his career was a futile attempt at running and hiding as he was found doing when his reign began?

LESSONS APPLIED

Has God assigned something for you to do? Perhaps it is to create or a purpose to accomplish. If you are like Saul, you have tried one or all of these three ploys to avoid the will of God: excuses, silence, and hiding. The hiding can take the form of busy-ness ("God, it is just not realistic for me to do Your will right now"), or silence ("If I don't volunteer or tell anyone about what God wants me to do, then God cannot use them to hold me accountable"), or excuses ("I don't have the education, time, or money to do that; I hope God gives it to someone else to do. After all, my kids need me"). I suppose we can boil all three down into one and that is trying to hide from God, using our thinking to generate excuses that will soothe and eventually sear our conscience.

Are you hiding? If you are, you have been found, just like Saul was found. God knows where you are and He has sent me to bring you out. You have something to do only you can do, so I suggest you get over the excuses, change your thinking, open your mouth, and accept the anointing that is yours. One word of caution: Don't act like you are doing God a favor as you come out of hiding. If you don't deal with your fear and rebellion, then your entire "career," like that of Saul, will be one of the reluctant disciple who must be coerced into obedience and that will not be beneficial for those around you—or for you.

Week #41

Proper Perspective

I have often written about the practice of false humility and the harm it does to your purpose and productivity. When you act like or deny the fact that you can do something well (false humility), you are talking yourself out of its importance and of your urgent need to do (or be) it more. While it seems spiritual to act with a lack of urgency, passivity, and self-deprecation, it often hinders, and can even thwart, God's ability to use you. There is a well-known quote from the Scottish poet Robert Burns, which states:

"Oh that the gods
The gift would gi'e us
To see ourselves
As others see us"

Often we think of the need to see ourselves as others see us when we are acting inappropriately, which does happen from time to time. I contend, however, that it is more important for us to see ourselves as others see us where our strengths and purpose are concerned, and not just in our sin and weakness. Can you see how this change of thinking can unlock your power to be and then act according to who God made you to be?

MIGHTY WARRIOR

When the Lord appeared to Gideon in Judges 6, notice how he greeted Gideon: "The Lord is with you, mighty warrior" (Judges 6:12). The interesting thing is that Gideon was not acting like a mighty warrior at the time; he was cowering in fear as he was threshing wheat in a spot hidden from his enemies. Gideon went on to engage in false humility, telling the Lord: "Pardon me, my lord," Gideon replied, "but how can I save Israel? My clan is the weakest in Manasseh, and I am the least in my family" (Judges 6:15). Something tells me you have reacted just as Gideon did; I know I have, too.

God had something to do that only Gideon could do and God saw it; he did not, either because he could not or he refused. At this point, you may say, "Well, that was what God saw and He knows everything." But often when God sees it (the "it" being your giftedness, power, or potential), others do as well. Later in the story, here is what someone said as they interpreted a dream another person had dreamt:

> "Gideon arrived just as a man was telling a friend his dream. 'I had a dream,' he was saying. 'A round loaf of barley bread came tumbling into the Midianite camp. It struck the tent with such force that the tent overturned and collapsed.' His friend responded, *This can be nothing other than the sword of Gideon son of Joash, the Israelite.* God has given the Midianites and the whole camp into his hands'" (Judges 7:13-14, emphasis added).

It wasn't just God who saw Gideon's power and potential; others saw it as well.

OTHERS SEE IT

There are times when you need to see yourself as others do when you are misbehaving. It is more important, however, that others see you in the power of your purpose—and that you listen to what they have to say. Paul wrote about this matter when he said: "For by the grace given me I say to every one of you: Do not think of yourself more highly than you ought, but rather think of yourself with sober judgment, in accordance with the faith God has distributed to each of you" (Romans 12:3). He warned his readers not to think more highly of themselves than is appropriate but did say they should accurately assess themselves.

Are you dismissing your power because you have been taught it's the spiritual thing to do? Has it caused you to be passive instead of aggressive in the revealed will of God for your life? Maybe this week you need to harken to prophetic words, or seek out a trusted mentor, or listen to the encouragement others have been or are trying to give you. Whatever it takes, I urge you to stop thinking false humility is spiritual and get about the work of accurately assessing the importance and power that God in His sovereign will has chosen to bestow upon you for His purpose and glory.

Week #42

Strengths and Weaknesses

I'm an advocate for functioning in your strengths as often as possible rather than spending time trying to improve your weaknesses. It makes no sense to me that God would give you a gift, which would be a strength of sorts, and then not want you to use it. If you have the strength or gift of singing, for example, you may want to sing a solo in front of your congregation. If you don't have it, then you shouldn't sing. That's pretty simple. Once I was reflecting on what Paul said and trying to resolve it regarding this issue of strengths and weaknesses:

> Three times I pleaded with the Lord to take it away from me. But he said to me, "My grace is sufficient for you, for my power is made perfect in weakness." Therefore I will boast all the more gladly about my weaknesses, so that Christ's power may rest on me. That is why, for Christ's sake, I delight in weaknesses, in insults, in hardships, in persecutions, in difficulties. For when I am weak, then I am strong (2 Corinthians 12:8-10).

Until I conducted a purpose seminar in my local church, I did not know how to resolve this seeming contradiction between exalting in weakness and functioning in strength. In the seminar, we were discussing how purpose is the answer to your "what?" question: "What should I do with my life?" Often we derail our consideration of the "what" by thinking about the "how" question: "How will I support myself and my family by doing this? How will it all work out? How can I possibly do this at my age (young or old)?" It's important that we unlock the power of our thinking where our strengths are concerned, otherwise we will always be ambivalent or double-minded about how and how often to go about expressing them.

I had the words *what* and *how* on the white board when one of the young ladies in the seminar offered this perspective: "It seems that the *what* is your strength, but the *how* is your weakness. We must accept the *what* but then trust the Lord for the *how*." And I thought, "Wow!"

Look back at what Paul wrote above. His weakness was the *how* of his purpose to the Gentiles. He experienced persecution and difficulties while people were insulting him, yet he was clear on the *what* he was to do. It was the *how* that was his challenge. He faced opposition on every front including his own physical limitations that sapped his energy. He was always clear on the *what*; it was the *how* that was his weakness. And it was in his weakness that the Lord was exalted.

Paul saw that he was in his best position for success when he was in his purpose while also facing his limitations, trusting the Lord to somehow make a way. And God always did make a way, even when he was in prison or on a sinking ship. When the ship was going down, Paul was fulfilling his purpose of taking the gospel to the Gentiles by witnessing to the ship's Gentile crew.

This kind of thinking is vital in your quest for purpose, for if you are going to face life's difficulties, you must do so from a position of purpose strength. When you go before the Lord for help to fulfill the purpose He assigned you, He *must* help You if He wants results—which of course He does. And from your position of the *how* weakness, He will help you fulfill your *what*.

Week #43

Fear Hunt

I regularly meet with people to talk about purpose and creativity. In most cases if not all, I find fear is holding them back in some way. What's more, most don't recognize the fear because it disguises itself so well. I have found this true in my own life, so let's talk about fear and how it locks up the power of your thinking and how you can find freedom.

WHERE IS IT?

For many years, I have assumed fear is somewhere lurking in my mind, so therefore I actively search for it, turning over the rocks, so to speak, in my heart and mind looking for the scorpions of fear that live below. I am no longer in denial but living in reality that fear is my constant companion. I must recognize it, bring it to the light of day, and confront it or else fear will continue to rob me of my opportunities. So I go on a fear hunt, saying to myself, "Where is it? I know it's here somewhere? Aha, there it is!"

What am I afraid of? You name it. I'm afraid of what others think. I'm afraid I don't have enough time to do something. I'm afraid I don't have time to do something well. I'm afraid I may miss the Lord by doing something. I'm afraid I will miss the Lord by ***not*** doing something. I'm afraid I won't have the finances to do something I want to do. You get the idea. You may think I am strange or unusual, but based on my experience, you have the same struggle. What's more, you are probably in denial that you do.

FEAR'S ORIGINS

We get our fears from our parents going all the way back to Adam and Eve. When Adam and Eve sinned, what did they do? They hid. And why did they hide? They hid because they were afraid:

> Then the man and his wife heard the sound of the Lord God as he was walking in the garden in the cool of the day, and they hid from the Lord God among the trees of the garden. But the Lord God called to the man, "Where are you?" He answered, "I heard you in the garden, and *I was afraid because I was naked; so I hid*" (Genesis 3:8-10, emphasis added).

WHAT TO DO WITH IT

I want you to do this week what I am doing: Assume fear is present in your life and go looking for it. It's cleverly disguised as being rational or spiritual and it can and does make a convincing case that it really isn't fear. Don't buy into it! Confront it for what it is, for until you know and accept the truth, the truth can't set you free. Knowing it's fear is the first step to courage and it will set you free to think big thoughts and set bold goals.

Once you find the fear, consider what it has cost you and then take action to counteract the effects of the fear. If you're like me, you will like the results of looking for the fear so much that you will no longer wait for it to knock you on the side of the head or rob you of your joy before you deal with it. Instead, you will go looking for it, knowing it's the great enemy of purpose and creativity that has cost you much in the way of productivity and purposeful living.

Week #44

Purpose Food

When I meet with people for some purpose coaching, I often ask them, "What can you do that causes you to lose track of time and perhaps even miss a meal?" They think and can generally come up with some scenario—being in church, going to a sporting event, reading a book. That then leads to a discussion of how that activity may be related to their purpose. Your purpose can often be so second nature to you that take it for granted, thinking it is nothing special. If you are going to unlock the power of your thinking, you must begin to see what you do that comes naturally as more than just something you learned how to do along the way of life. It's your purpose.

I started asking that question in my sessions because of something I saw in John's gospel about Jesus and the woman at the well, which we discussed in an earlier chapter. It's worth examining one more time.

LUNCH

In John's account, Jesus and the disciples were tired and hungry from travel, so the disciples went into town to buy lunch while Jesus rested at Jacob's well in Samaria. This was not a usual rest stop for Jews since they did not like to mix with Samaritans. While Jesus was resting, a woman came by to draw water. This was not a usual time to draw, for it was already in the heat of the day and most women would have taken care of that duty early in the morning. Perhaps Jesus was suspicious as to why this woman was coming so late, so He engaged her in conversation.

During their talk, the woman tried to debate Jesus about religion, but He pressed her for information about her personal life and ultimately revealed Himself to her as the Messiah she had been alluding to in her comments. At that point, she ran off to tell her neighbors that she had met a man (I doubt if anyone was surprised at that, for she had "met" many men in her lifetime)—just as the disciples returned with food. They were shocked to find that Jesus was no longer hungry and urged him to eat:

> Meanwhile his disciples urged him, "Rabbi, eat something." But he said to them, "I have food to eat that you know nothing about." Then his disciples said to each other, "Could someone have brought him food?" "My food," said Jesus, "is to do the will of him who sent me and to finish his work" (John 4:31-34).

PURPOSE HUNGER

Jesus was no longer hungry because He was exhilarated from His encounter with the woman. He had fulfilled His purpose when he spoke with her, which was "to seek and save the lost" (see Luke 19:10) and that fulfillment had satisfied His hunger. If Jesus had purpose food, so do you. What do you do that you can miss a meal? Is it painting a canvas or a room? Counseling a friend? Traveling on a plane? The answers to those questions are important clues in your quest to find your purpose. Even pursuing the answers can cause you to miss a meal, and that in itself is significant.

This whole scenario makes me think of Deuteronomy 8:3, which Jesus Himself quoted to the devil in Matthew 4: "He humbled you, causing you to hunger and then feeding you with manna, which neither you nor your ancestors had known, to teach you that man does not live on bread alone but on every word that comes from the mouth of the Lord." This week, spend some time asking and answering that question about what is sometimes better for you than eating and I'm confident you will have not only food for thought that will unlock your thinking but ultimately food for purpose.

Week #45

Purpose Prayer

In 1981, I found my purpose while I was recovering from a poorly conceived and failed business venture with some other men. One morning while begging God to somehow save the business, I asked the question, "If You did not create me to start this business, what *did* You create me to do?" Mind you, I was not looking for information, I was venting my frustration to God, trying desperately to stave off embarrassment, failure, and financial loss.

To my surprise, I made a discovery that morning—I found my purpose! God answered my question and while I did not realize the true value of what I had found at the time, I had stumbled on my purpose that would continue to shape my life and the lives of many others. That one thought unlocked an entire series of thoughts that has directed my life and development since then. In 1991, I began to teach and write about purpose, and the rest is history, as they say. But it's not all history for the best is yet to come, for there is more interest today in purpose than at any time since 1991. In 1995, I wrote my first book about purpose. In 2001, I founded my company PurposeQuest. One purpose thought was the key to unlocking many more purpose thoughts. So let's talk about it a little more in this chapter, shall we?

THE MAIN REASON

The main reason you don't know your purpose is that you have not asked and *kept on* asking until you found or understood the answer. Purpose requires a different way of thinking, for you have been conditioned to think or ask about your career. However, purpose is the essence of who you are. It's not about money, perks, or promotions. It's the song God put in your heart to sing in a way that only you can do. That's the reason it's so important to ask and keep on seeking God for your purpose—so you can get new thoughts to unlock your purpose power.

When I think of seeking the Lord, I'm always drawn by the call to prayer found in Proverbs 2:3-5: "Indeed, if you *call out* for insight and *cry aloud* for understanding, and if you *look* for it as for silver and *search* for it as for hidden treasure, then you will understand the fear of the Lord and find the knowledge of God" (emphasis added). Notice the active, almost aggressive nature of seeking prayer that Proverbs suggests. You must *call, cry, look* and *search*, and then and only then will you find that for which you are looking.

PURPOSE PRAYER

If I guaranteed that there was buried treasure in your backyard and you dug one hole and didn't find it, would you give up? Probably not. You would dig again and dig deeper until you found the promised bounty. That is how it is with purpose. You have it, but it's often buried and hidden so you must search through the wrong thinking in your mind to find the hidden treasure, not giving up until you have it. Why can that be such a difficult process? I'm not sure of all the reasons, but I do know the more effort you put into finding it, the more valuable and precious it will be once you do.

Are you ready to do some praying and seeking if not to find your purpose, then to understand how to fulfill it? Are you ready to confront and change the thoughts about yourself and your future that will lead to exciting new discoveries? I trust you are ready and willing to go for it, and will not stop until you have reached your objective. You can't be passive if you're going to pray effective purpose prayers so I encourage you to step up your intensity and watch and see what God does. It was effective for me and I'm sure it will be for you, too.

Week #46

Purpose Thoughts

In the last two chapters, we have looked at purpose food and purpose prayer. It seems only fitting that I write one more chapter to complete this trinity of purpose insights, so "purpose thoughts" seems just as good as any—especially since our theme is how to unlock the power in your thoughts. Let me share some purpose thoughts with you in random order of importance that have the potential to take root in your mind and bear abundant fruit.

THE THOUGHTS

1. Purpose is more relevant than when I began teaching it 30 years ago. Why? Because there are more opportunities available today than back then. When there are so many things you *can* do, you must ask more than ever what it is that you *should* do.
2. The number one reason why more people don't know their purpose is because they don't ask and keep on asking until they get an answer.
3. The number two reason why more people don't know their purpose is because they try to figure out too quickly *how* they can make money or a career from it. Thoughts about career path, salary, and benefits hinder or thwart emerging purpose thoughts.
4. The number three reason why more people don't know their purpose is because they are afraid, not of failure, but of success. Meditate on that for a moment.
5. The younger generation is not as interested in purpose as I would have thought. They are interested in

service and meaning, which emanate from purpose. Because they have seen purpose kidnapped by salary and career interests, they react to the concept of purpose for the wrong reasons.

6. Women continue to be the main consumers of my purpose message, probably because purpose has been denied them for so long.
7. I maintain that motherhood is a *role* and not a *purpose*. Seldom is anyone's purpose defined in terms of exclusively serving or helping another person, unless that person has special needs due to a physical or mental challenge.
8. It's never too early or too late in life to pursue purpose.
9. When I reached my fifties, I thought my development was pretty much over and I would do what I had been doing, hopefully a little better or for more money. To my surprise, that decade of my life held my greatest growth years.
10. I get more questions and sometimes opposition when I teach about doing what you love and what gives you joy than anything else I teach. That always surprises me.
11. When I started teaching purpose, I thought every church in the world (well, at least in the U.S.) would want their people to hear the message. They have not and pastors continue to misunderstand and even oppose it.
12. If I could help churches get more volunteers to usher, work in the nursey, or sing in the choir, I would be a busy and probably wealthy man.

If any of the points above stood out to you, I would encourage you to think about them. One way to unlock the power of your thinking is to introduce new thoughts and reflect on them, perhaps even recording your reflections in your journal. For example, if number nine above intrigues you, then examine your thoughts about growing older and see where your assumptions are limiting your potential as you approach that age. Then think new thoughts that will unlock your thinking that may cause you to go back to school, change careers, or pick up an old or new hobby, all because you unlocked your potential by unlocking your thinking.

Week #47

Living in Your Dream

Let's take a look at Genesis Joseph in Genesis and see what we can learn from him about how to unlock our thinking power. Joseph was a man of purpose who saved the world while also saving his family from famine. If you have time, read Joseph's full story from Genesis 37-50, but if you don't want to take the time, let me summarize it for you.

THE PROCESS

When Joseph was 17 years old, he had two dreams, both of which his family interpreted to mean that one day they would all bow down to Joseph as the family leader. This brought a rebuke from his father but active hatred from his brothers, who eventually sold him into slavery. Joseph was carried down to Egypt where he became the servant of a man named Potiphar. Joseph thrived while serving Potiphar, but Mrs. Potiphar had romantic ideas about the two of them and tried to prevail upon Joseph to sleep with her. When Joseph refused, she lied and accused him of rape.

Mr. Potiphar was angry and sent Joseph to prison, where Joseph again excelled in service and leadership. After correctly interpreting the dreams of two fellow inmates who were Pharaoh's servants, Joseph was eventually brought before Pharaoh to interpret Pharaoh's dreams. The dreams indicated the world would suffer a famine and Joseph saw in the dreams a plan by which the world could have food during the seven years of lack.

By the time all this happened, Joseph was 30 years of age (see Genesis 41:46) and had been in Egypt for 13 years. After all that time, he was promoted to second-in-command under Pharaoh and gave oversight to the seven years of plenty when grain was stored for the famine. That is when the story gets even more interesting.

LIVING THE DREAM

Joseph's father Jacob thought Joseph was dead while his brothers who knew the truth were simply glad he was gone. Eventually, however, Joseph's family was affected by the worldwide famine so they went down to Egypt to buy food. Joseph saw and recognized them but they did not recognize him because they thought he was dead—they had believed the lie they had told. Have you believed something false for so long that you now believe it to be true? That is an area of your thinking that certainly needs unlocked.

Genesis makes a startling statement about Joseph: "Then he [Joseph] remembered his dreams about them [his brothers]" (Genesis 42:9). Since the brothers came in the second year of the famine, Joseph was 39 years old when he recognized them and also remembered the dream. If you don't remember your dreams from last night, how did Joseph remember his dreams for twenty-two years?

He remembered them because he "lived" in them. He lived in them in his mind while on the long trip after being sold into slavery. He lived in them during those early years serving Potiphar and in the later years in prison. He remembered them during the first years of Pharaoh's favor when he married a foreign woman and started a family. Therefore, when the brothers came in after twenty-two years of believing a lie while Joseph was living in his dream world, Joseph saw his dream become a reality.

The implications for you are clear. If your "dream" tarries, live in it and you can do so by thinking about it. Visualize the dream and see yourself in the midst of its fulfillment. Hold onto that dream no matter what and no matter how far away from its reality you may be. You will unlock the power of your thinking when are selective as to what you think about and choose to focus on what Paul wrote to the Philippians:

> Do not be anxious about anything, but in every situation, by prayer and petition, with thanksgiving, present your requests to God. And the peace of God, which

> transcends all understanding, will guard your hearts and your minds in Christ Jesus. Finally, brothers and sisters, whatever is true, whatever is noble, whatever is right, whatever is pure, whatever is lovely, whatever is admirable—if anything is excellent or praiseworthy—think about such things. Whatever you have learned or received or heard from me, or seen in me—put it into practice. And the God of peace will be with you (Philippians 4:6-9).

When Joseph's brothers came in to beg for bread, Joseph was ready to assume his place in the real-life version of his dreams and they became a reality. His brothers and family did indeed bow down and recognize him as their leader. Your dreams will become a reality too, but only if you think about them today so you can live in them tomorrow.

Week #48

Starting Points

I heard someone say that people are rational beings who do irrational things. After almost 50 years as a pastor and observing all kinds of strange behavior, I'm inclined to agree with that statement. I have reflected on it often and would like to share some conclusions with you since they are pertinent to our discussion of our thinking and its power.

IRRATIONALITY

Irrational behavior has its start in our minds with how we are thinking. In Mark 3:1-5, we read

> Another time Jesus went into the synagogue, and a man with a shriveled hand was there. Some of them were looking for a reason to accuse Jesus, so they watched him closely to see if he would heal him on the Sabbath. Jesus said to the man with the shriveled hand, "Stand up in front of everyone." Then Jesus asked them, "Which is lawful on the Sabbath: to do good or to do evil, to save life or to kill?" But they remained silent. He looked around at them in anger and, deeply distressed at their stubborn hearts, said to the man, "Stretch out your hand." He stretched it out, and his hand was completely restored.

How often have you said, "Lord, if I had a sign to confirm your will, I would do it." In this story, the Pharisees witnessed a magnificent and startling sign: A man's withered hand was un-withered before their very eyes. What was their response? We read in Mark 3:6: "Then the Pharisees went out and began to plot with the Herodians how they might kill Jesus."

They saw Jesus perform a miracle and their response to it

was He had to die. That's irrational and their problem was what I am going to refer to as their starting point. Their starting point was their assumption of incorrect thought that they knew all there was to know about the Sabbath. They further thought it was their job to protect the Sabbath on God's behalf from violators. When they saw the miracle, they evaluated it based on an irrational or incorrect starting point. From then on, they acted in a rational manner, for if they were correct (which of course they were not), then the rational thing to do was punish Jesus for His offense.

STARTING POINT EXAMPLES

My point is that you have starting points and they impact how you rationally carry out your life and ministry. Here are some examples:

- **Starting point:** I don't have time to write a book." **Result:** You don't even try. **Truth:** You have all the time in the world (24 hours every day) but are probably using the lack of time as a front for your fear.
- **Starting point:** "I don't have money to give." **Result:** You don't give, God doesn't bless you, so you have even less to give. **Truth:** Even a small "widow's mite" can have an effect on God and the situation into which you are giving.

Where are you rationally living in a pattern that began with an irrational starting point? The only way to find out is to continually challenge your thinking where starting points are concerned. You don't have time to write a book? How is it then that I have written as many as I have? (Rational thinking says, "Get some sleep," but that is actually irrational because I can do all things through Christ who strengthens me.)

You don't have money to give? How is it that you have $200 for cable television service? Because you have never challenged your "need" for so much television, you don't see how you can obey God's command to be generous. You are correct (rationally) that you don't have money to give—because you are wasting it on something to satisfy your own desires.

This week, challenge some of your starting points to see if they are passing as rational when they really are not. If they aren't, then if you change your "starting point," you will unlock the power of your thinking to think new thoughts and come to more rational starting points. Then those new thoughts will lead to new behaviors so you will be a rational being doing rational things.

Week #49

Run Like a Deer

I once served as a mentor for someone in their doctoral degree program, and we had weekly meetings. We discussed a variety of topics when during one session the student asked me a question that pertained to the phrase found in Habakkuk 3:19: "The Sovereign LORD is my strength; he makes my feet like the feet of a deer, he enables me to tread on the heights." I went home and turned to Habakkuk to research the context of the verse. I found that the prophet was waiting for Judah's enemies to invade as God had promised would happen as a consequence of Judah's waywardness. Here is the full context:

> I heard and my heart pounded, my lips quivered at the sound; decay crept into my bones, and my legs trembled. Yet I will wait patiently for the day of calamity to come on the nation invading us. Though the fig tree does not bud and there are no grapes on the vines, though the olive crop fails and the fields produce no food, though there are no sheep in the pen and no cattle in the stalls, yet I will rejoice in the Lord, I will be joyful in God my Savior. *The Sovereign Lord is my strength; he makes my feet like the feet of a deer, he enables me to tread on the heights* (Habakkuk 3:11-19, emphasis added).

Habakkuk was physically weak from the thought of the impending invasion, just like certain thoughts can weaken you. What's more, the prophet knew what would happen when the invasion came: Food would be short, there would be suffering and, ultimately, the invaders would be victorious. Despite the circumstances, however, Habakkuk like Nehemiah after him would proclaim that the Lord was his strength. Because of that reality and his choice to focus on that thought and not on the impending doom, Habakkuk likened his condition in the Lord to that of a deer.

DEER FACTS

What do we know about a deer? They are fast and can leap high into the air with graceful, elegant, effortless movement. Those characteristics are in deer because that is who God created them to be. That image of a deer bounding across a field or in the woods should be etched in your mind as an image of how we should be when we choose to put our faith in God. Earlier in his book, Habakkuk had included a phrase that became instrumental in New Testament teaching: "Behold, as for the proud one, His soul is not right within him; but the righteous will live by his faith" (Habakkuk 2:4 NASB).

God has created you to do great things that are not dependent on the circumstances in which you find yourself. God empowers you to run and tread on the heights if you live by faith. Does that describe your life? Are you running? Are you jumping? Is the Sovereign Lord your strength who empowers you to do more than you thought you could do and endure more difficulties than you imagined? Can you prosper and be productive, even in down times of famine and lack?

Reflect on this passage or perhaps on the entire book of Habakkuk in the coming week because we will look at the concept of deer in the next two chapters. The Lord directed the prophet to write down what the Lord was going to show him and that is good advice for you as well:

> Then the Lord answered me and said, "Record the vision and inscribe *it* on tablets, that the one who reads it may run. For the vision is yet for the appointed time; it hastens toward the goal and it will not fail. Though it tarries, wait for it; for it will certainly come, it will not delay" (Habakkuk 2:2-3 NASB).

Have your journal ready to record the vision God will give you concerning your life and purpose, and then begin to build a thought world around what He says. Your thoughts will then activate your deer-like qualities, and you will be ready to leap into new aspects of a purposeful life full of goals. Those will lead to wonderful end results that will glorify God and inspire you to climb to even greater faith and purpose heights.

Week #50

Drink Like a Deer

Habakkuk 3:19 states, "The Sovereign Lord is my strength; he makes my feet like the feet of a deer, he enables me to tread on the heights." Those words were first penned by David and can also be found in 2 Samuel 22:34 and Psalm 18:33. Obviously, Habakkuk had turned to the psalms in his distress and incorporated words that were particularly meaningful to him in his time of trouble. What verses are special to you in your own times of trouble? The psalms include one more passage that mentions deer, found in Psalm 42:

> As the deer pants for streams of water, so my soul pants for you, my God. My soul thirsts for God, for the living God. When can I go and meet with God? My tears have been my food day and night, while people say to me all day long, "Where is your God?" (Psalm 42:1-3).

TIMES OF TROUBLE

All the deer references speak to God's' ability to sustain you in times of trouble. In fact, God won't simply help you maintain or survive in tough times, He will cause you to thrive and stand strong. That is one of the reasons why tough times come: to prove that the work God has done in your life is for real and will stand not just during problems, but for all eternity. James also later wrote about God's work in your life during difficulties:

> Consider it pure joy, my brothers and sisters, whenever you face trials of many kinds, because you know that the testing of your faith produces perseverance. Let perseverance finish its work so that you may be mature and complete, not lacking anything (James 1:2-4).

The word "consider" is a thought word. James was telling his readers how to think about their trials and tests. There is a word to describe that process and it is called "framing." Framing is defined as follows: "the process of defining the context or issues that surround a problem or event in a way that serves to influence how the context or issues are seen and evaluated." James was telling us, "How you interpret or frame your trials will determine how you respond to them. If you see them as joy, then you will embrace them. If you think of them as an intrusion, you will oppose and fight them."

In Psalm 42, the psalmist used a vivid word picture to indicate our need for God in our problems. We must be like a thirsty deer that needs to find streams of water for its survival. It did not look for lemonade or some other beverage, for only water has what the deer needs. The same is true for us. In times of trouble, you don't need a vacation or some entertainment diversion. You don't need to read a self-help book. You need the Lord. If you frame your problem incorrectly, then you will think that a vacation is what you need. Jesus said He was like water and that all who thirsted should come to Him and drink (see John 7:37-38).

THE WOMAN AT THE WELL

The woman at the well had discovered that truth in John's gospel when she came to the well for water, but instead heard Jesus say, "Everyone who drinks this water will be thirsty again, but whoever drinks the water I give them will never thirst. Indeed, the water I give them will become in them a spring of water welling up to eternal life" (John 4:13-14). She had framed her problem as natural thirst, but Jesus saw the real problem as spiritual thirst. When she saw it properly, she acted appropriately.

If you are facing difficult times, is your thought that God is your source of sustenance and refreshment? Are you standing strong and drinking deeply of His word and His presence? James urged you not just to endure the trials, but to consider or think about them as a joyful experience because the end result will be a strengthening of your commitment to follow the Lord. During those trials, God will work things into you (and out of you) that are for your ultimate good.

I pray that you will think of yourself like a deer during this season of your life, standing firm in Him and drinking deeply of the encouragement He will give you in abundance. He will only be able to encourage you, however, if you frame your current situation with the right thoughts. Then when you seek Him, you will find Him to be the source of relief and strength in your distress—rather than some other diversion.

Week

#51

Fight Like a Deer

In the last two chapters, we have looked at several references to deer in the Old Testament and their characteristics that are to be part of a believer's faith thoughts repertoire. The first reference was about speed and agility as you carry out your God-assigned purpose. The second was about thirsting for the Lord as a deer would thirst for water, requiring a drink regularly to replenish supplies due to an active lifestyle. In this chapter, let's look at a third reference found in both 2 Samuel 22 and Psalm 18, and that reference is to the deer as a fighter. You didn't know that deer fight? Well, then consider yourself about to be educated on the subject.

TRAINED FOR BATTLE

Psalm 18 is actually first found in its entirety in 2 Samuel 22 where this introduction is included: "David sang to the Lord the words of this song when the Lord delivered him from the hand of all his enemies and from the hand of Saul" (2 Samuel 22:1). The same heading is in the Psalm 18 heading. The context for the deer reference in this psalm is found in verses 32 to 36:

> It is God who arms me with strength and keeps my way secure. He makes my feet like the feet of a deer; he causes me to stand on the heights. He trains my hands for battle; my arms can bend a bow of bronze. You make your saving help my shield, and your right hand sustains me; your help has made me great. You provide a broad path for my feet, so that my ankles do not give way.

I exaggerated a bit in my opening paragraph for deer are not known for their fighting. David used the simile of a deer to describe his sure-footed ways in battle, a situation in which you do not want to stumble and fall so your enemy can take advantage of your vulnerable position. Just like David, God wants us to battle, but our battle takes place first and foremost in our minds. Paul wrote,

> For though we live in the world, we do not wage war as the world does. The weapons we fight with are not the weapons of the world. On the contrary, they have divine power to demolish strongholds. We demolish arguments and every pretension that sets itself up against the knowledge of God, and we take captive every thought to make it obedient to Christ (2 Corinthians 10:3-5).

A MIND WAR

When you have a thought, you can dwell on that thought until it becomes so embedded that it is a way of life for you, something from which you will not deviate or even listen to something that seems to contradict it. We have examined that reality throughout this book and also addressed how to avoid or escape it. For example, let's consider a common saying that isn't quite true, but sounds true: "God helps those who help themselves." When you think and believe it, it can become such a stronghold that you refuse to allow God to do anything for you, choosing instead to do it for yourself. The same can be true for a false doctrine like Islam or Scientology. Once that doctrine gets a hold in the mind, it can become a stronghold and must be forcibly removed.

You have some thoughts that are holding you back in pursuing your purpose. You may have a stronghold that you don't travel well, and as a result, you don't travel at all. You may have a stronghold that you are too old to learn or too young to be used by God, and as a result you don't read or try to fulfill your purpose. The point of all this is that you are to be as active and energetic as a deer in fighting the thoughts that are holding you back, replacing them with thoughts that will serve God's purpose in your life.

As we close, I hope you are convinced your mind is the

main battleground that will either empower or hinder you from effectively serving the Lord. It's time you stopped accepting your business-as-usual thinking and challenged your thoughts to see if they are conducive to action while also consistent with God's standards. If they are not, then God expects you to fight with the strength, grace, and speed of a deer and He will empower and sustain you to do so—unless your thoughts resist the process. With His help, you will be able to achieve the great things He has in mind for you that your own mind can either accept and enhance—or oppose.

Week #52

Your Assumptions

As we close, let's examine one last Old Testament story about a man named Naaman who was stricken with a dreaded ancient disease: leprosy. We read,

> Now Naaman was commander of the army of the king of Aram. He was a great man in the sight of his master and highly regarded, because through him the LORD had given victory to Aram. He was a valiant soldier, but he had leprosy (2 Kings 5:1).

As Providence would have it, there was someone in Naaman's household who had the answer to his dilemma:

> Now bands of raiders from Aram had gone out and had taken captive a young girl from Israel, and she served Naaman's wife. She said to her mistress, "If only my master would see the prophet who is in Samaria! He would cure him of his leprosy" (2 Kings 5:2-3).

As we will learn, Naaman made some specific assumptions about how his healing would occur and that almost cost him enjoying the solution to his problem because his thinking was all wrong.

"I THOUGHT"

When Naaman arrived in Israel, he went directly to the prophet's home:

> So Naaman went with his horses and chariots and stopped at the door of Elisha's house. Elisha sent a messenger to say to him, "Go, wash yourself seven times in the Jordan, and your flesh will be restored and you will be cleansed" (2 Kings 5:9-10).

These instructions were not what Naaman had in mind, for he was used to battles and excitement and honor and prestige. In this case, the prophet did not even feel it necessary to meet with him, so Naaman was offended and insulted:

> But Naaman went away angry and said, "*I thought* that he would surely come out to me and stand and call on the name of the Lord his God, wave his hand over the spot and cure me of my leprosy. Are not Abana and Pharpar, the rivers of Damascus, better than all the waters of Israel? Couldn't I wash in them and be cleansed?" So he turned and went off in a rage (2 Kings 5:11-12, emphasis added).

Naaman "thought" his healing *had* to take place in the way he had anticipated. Have you ever gone off in a rage because your expectations were not met because your assumptions were wrong?

RIGHT THINKING LED TO RIGHT ACTION

Fortunately for Naaman, he had other servants in his entourage who had more wisdom and better thinking on the matter than he did:

> Naaman's servants went to him and said, "My father, if the prophet had told you to do some great thing, would you not have done it? How much more, then, when he tells you, 'Wash and be cleansed'!" So he went down and dipped himself in the Jordan seven times, as the man of God had told him, and his flesh was restored and became clean like that of a young boy (2 Kings 5:13-14).

Naaman almost missed his opportunity for wholeness because his assumptions were unrealistic. His military might and success had no relevance in this situation. The same is true for you. Even if you are a mature believer, you can still take wrong actions because of wrong thinking. Ultimately, Naaman had to humble himself and admit that he was in the wrong and his servants were correct. In all probability, that was the reason God had sent him the instructions he did through the prophet—so Naaman would show a little humility, for we know that God gives grace to the humble but resists the proud.

Do you have proud thoughts that lead to prideful actions? Are you so enamored with your assumptions of how God and others should act that you miss what He or they may be doing when it isn't according to your predetermined plan? If you do, then God can't help you because your thinking is askew. He is confronting your pride by doing something in a way you never expected. That means you must work to change your thinking and assumptions if you want to see God move on your behalf.

As we close this book, I hope you have learned how important it is to think about what you think about. It's necessary to challenge your starting points and assumptions and then realign your thinking wherever and whenever it does not line up with faith. If you have the courage to face your fears and accept that you play an important role in what God can and wants to do through you, then you will release your thoughts to flow and work as God intended.

God is not looking for robots or passive radio receivers that only activate or function when they get a signal from heaven. He wants you to renew your mind so you can actively participate with Him in the process of finding and fulfilling your purpose. I hope the lessons in this book have helped you toward that end and will continue to help you as you engage in the lifelong work of unlocking the power of your thinking.

Appendix

Journaling Tips

Catherine Franz has taught journaling for the last 15 years, including two US Presidents and First Ladies, and hundreds of workshops internationally. http://www.catherinefranz.com

Blog: http://abundance.blogs.com/intothelight

Article Source: http://EzineArticles.com/?expert=Catherine_Franz

There are no hard-set rules for keeping a journal. How often you write, time you spend, and how rigorously you maintain a regular journaling schedule are matters of personal choice and circumstance. Therefore, it is important to find what works for you.

Allow me to provide nine guidelines I promote:

1. **Having a regular journaling time builds routine and discipline.** Journaling isn't necessarily about what you write; it's about just getting your thoughts out to build emotional balance. Find a time of day that feels good for you. Return at this time as often as possible even if you don't think you have anything to say, you're tired, or not quite awake. Start by just recording a quote you remembered, or a mantra you're currently using now for change. Maybe even a list of items you need to do that day or the next day. The process only requires a starting place. The rest will flow naturally. Everyone needs personal time to process his or her thinking. It builds emotional intelligence (EQ). Allow yourself, be gentle with yourself, and give yourself permission to be emotionally balanced.

2. **Set your space up for success**. Would you prefer your environment to be quiet? Maybe you need hustle and bustle around you. Do you prefer specific music or certain writing materials? I

like to have my favorite blanket around me when thinking through personal stuff. I like to write about business stuff in a noisy place. I like to write about marketing in McDonalds with the smell of french fries and grease. Where are yours?

3. **Develop a centering ritual**. By associating journaling with another pleasurable habit, you can strengthen your journal practice and create an atmosphere of self-nurturing. The ritual can include a glass of wine, tea or coffee. It can be after a phone with someone. It can begin with a certain piece of music. Maybe meditation, deep breathing exercises, or prayer centers you. I have a list of ways to center typed and taped in the front of each journal. I go down the list and start with the one that feels right at that time.

4. **Begin with a prompt**. Maybe you want to focus on particular type of personal development change and a prompt brings you into that focus faster. Or maybe a general reflection prompt lights the spark plugs. For instance, "What am I feeling right now?" or "What's been on mind?" Journaling author Anais Nin suggests asking, "What feels vivid, warm, or near to you at the moment?"

5. **Write because you know there's a big benefit for you to do so**. Don't allow journaling to become an obligation or a chore. Allow yourself to give to yourself. Be kind and gentle during this process. Allow the experience to always been seen as possible no matter what pours onto the page. Don't demand more of yourself than you can give at the time. It's perfect. If you miss a day or several days, accept that journaling, like life, is imperfect, and goes on. Begin again when do have a chance. Beating yourself up for not journaling isn't going to help anyone, including you. No one is grading you. No one is measuring and tracking. Be kind to yourself. Remember, there are no rules.

6. **Create a positive feedback loop**. As you continue to use the journal as an opportunity to be with and learn about yourself, you will find that the practice gains a momentum all on its own. Discovering your own hidden depths piques your curiosity and stimulates you to continue, setting up a positive feedback loop between your conscious and unconscious mind. It opens the gaps

that fall in between space and time. It opens creativity, imagination, and possibilities.

7. **Emphasize the process and not the product**. An important purpose of journal writing is simply expressing and recording your thoughts and feelings. Focus on the thinking process. Keep the words flowing and stop being concerned about the result. If your journaling is about something specific, re-read. Allow room for editing if you choose. Be free to cross out words because you changed your mind and found a better one. Allow yourself to cross out paragraphs and rewrite them so they really mean what you say. This is all part of the thinking process. Every time you rewrite your pose, your growth triples. Use your journal as the raw material processing for more polished thinking.

8. **Learn from your experiences**. Set up a time to re-read your entries. It's good to see how far you've grown in your thinking. It re-enforces how you've changed and grown. It's a wonderful, personal way to pat you on the back from life. When you reread your material, look for patterns and correlations. What improved? What stayed the same? Learning from you is much gentler on self-esteem. Use objectivity to see a new perspective or hindsight lesson.

Relax, have fun, and laugh! Journal writing is its own reward. Once you get started, your journal will become a good friend. It's available whenever you need it. Day, night, home, in the car, or in a coffee shop. It's a 24/7 friend and is always ready to love you back if you let it.

Your journal loves you for just being you.

About John W. Stanko

John founded a personal and leadership development company, called *PurposeQuest*, in 2001 and today travels the world to speak, consult and inspire leaders and people everywhere. From 2001-2008, he spent six months a year in Africa and still enjoys visiting and working on that continent. Most recently, John founded Urban Press, a publishing service designed to tell stories of the city, from the city and to the city. John is the author of 50 books.

Keep in Touch with John W. Stanko

www.purposequest.com
www.johnstanko.us
www.stankobiblestudy.com
www.stankomondaymemo.com

or via email at johnstanko@gmail.com

John also does extensive relief and community development work in Kenya. You can see some of his projects at www.purposequest.com/contributions

PurposeQuest International
PO Box 8882
Pittsburgh, PA 15221-0882

Additional Titles by John W. Stanko

Unlocking the Power of Your Creativity
Unlocking the Power of Your Productivity
Unlocking the Power of Your Purpose
Unlocking the Power of You
Unlocking the Power of Your Faith